THE LAST BOOK ...

DR. JAMES J. HAVILAND

Copyright © 2023 Dr. James J. Haviland.

All rights reserved. No part of this book may be reproduced, stored, or transmitted by any means—whether auditory, graphic, mechanical, or electronic—without written permission of both publisher and author, except in the case of brief excerpts used in critical articles and reviews. Unauthorized reproduction of any part of this work is illegal and is punishable by law.

ISBN: 979-8-89031-213-6 (sc)
ISBN: 979-8-89031-214-3 (hc)
ISBN: 979-8-89031-215-0 (e)

Because of the dynamic nature of the Internet, any web addresses or links contained in this book may have changed since publication and may no longer be valid. The views expressed in this work are solely those of the author and do not necessarily reflect the views of the publisher, and the publisher hereby disclaims any responsibility for them.

One Galleria Blvd., Suite 1900, Metairie, LA 70001
1-888-421-2397

Also By Dr. James J. Haviland

This Book Is No Joke!
The Critical Role of Humor In Communication

Bridging the Communication Gap
Bringing Diverse Personalities Together for Successful Engagement

Bridging the Communication Gap
Bringing Diverse Personalities Together for Successful Engagement
2nd Edition

This book is dedicated to my amazing wife Alicia,
our seven sensational children Wade, Adam,
Chelsea, Brittany, Reid, Blake and Chase.
Fantastic in-laws Lena, Melissa, Chad, Lexie, Laci and Marisa.
And our dazzling dozen grandchildren; Natasha, Preston, Veda,
Ever, Rhett, Arah, Knox, Ryker, Nash, Lily, Elise and Ivy.

CONTENTS

Preface ix
Introduction xxiii

PART I: THE PERFECT STORM

Partisanship 3
Narcissism 7
Technology 12
Litigation 14

PART II: COMMUNICATION IN THE 21ST CENTURY

Section 1	Engagement 19
Section 2	Perceived Value.. 39
Section 3	The Ivory Tower... 44
Section 4	Leadership: Success/Wealth/Fame 49
Section 5	A Sense of Humor 55
Section 6	Risk/Self-Esteem 73
Section 7	Critical Choices 78
Section 8	Emotional Tones 89

Section 9	Flow 103
Section 10	Change Avoidance 106
Section 11	The Joy of Independent Thought and Choice 114
Section 12	The Influence of Technology 119

PART III: DIFFUSING CONFLICT

Section 13	The Ability to Diffuse Conflict 127
Section 14	Humor Its Origin and Power 139
Section 15	Humor. What Happened to it? 149
Section 16	Decisions and Consequences 159
Section 17	Restoring Inner Confidence 174
Section 18	The Aftermath 186

Epilogue 189

PART IV: 'ON MY WAY PROJECT'

On My Way Project 197
Appendix A 201
Appendix B 204
Appendix C 207

PART V: RESOURCES

Resources 211

PREFACE

The Last Book ... is considered to be a work of speculative fiction. It is a warning to cherish the freedoms that you currently have, however be aware of the insidious transformation that is taking place in the culture as it relates to communication. In some respects, **The Last Book ...** is a battle-field manual addressing the survival techniques that will be necessary to navigate this global transition in communication. In order to survive "the perfect storm" and create working relationships with your peers and move from success to significance a new skill-set is required.

At the time the first edition of *Bridging the Communication Gap* was released in 2015, I had no idea of the books accuracy in foreshadowing the events that were to take place during the next five years. Both the first edition, and the second edition, focus on the development and success of the individual reader. There is no focus on the overall social or political agendas that have developed recently within our culture. The focus in **The Last Book ... remains on the sole reader.**

The foreshadowing existed by drawing attention to the importance of effective communication and its' apparent decline. The only issue is, I underestimated the magnitude of decline and polarization of opinions that would occur as it relates to communication during this past one-half of a decade. Communication didn't become more difficult, it ceased. Perhaps I should have taken notice of comedian Martin Lawrence's warning in 1992, "Talk to the hand," and realized it was a precursor of what was to come. It was, and is, worse than I had imagined it would be. So, I congratulate myself on my ability to foreshadow. However, we now face a far greater problem as it relates to effective communication. The polarization of opinions, in conjunction with the depersonalization of society due to the pandemic, have created the ingredients for a perfect storm. What form will that storm take?

I introduce the storm-analogy in the realm of communications because there are so many similarities between storms and poor communication. Both have warning signs that are frequently ignored, often with harsh consequences. Prior to a storm, the sky has a greenish tint, wall clouds develop and heavy hail slices through the atmosphere. In communication, it may ignite around arguing over the crowd size at an event. Storms vary in size from hailstorms to typhoons churning at 190 MPH. In communication, the storm may range from silly nicknames to unceremonious dismissals. Both have a considerable span of destruction as an end result to individual reputations and property.

Both storms and breakdowns in communications, require specific circumstances to take place in order to become deadly. In a storm, it requires certain atmospheric moisture, lift and instability. In breakdowns in communication, it requires a culture of self-obsessed, narcissistic individuals influenced by fear and manipulation.

I yield to the power and influence of these variables that exist within our society and I will make no attempt to defend or refute their existence. It is, what it is. Nor is this going to evolve into a treatise on political parties and their respective positions. I'll leave that up to the political pundits, of which there are plenty. Long ago, I declared my independent status until they take public money out of elections and impose term limits. I will stay focused on the individual; without party affiliation and steps they may take to ensure their personal success.

My focus will be on the reader, the future generations to come, and how they may be touched by the insights gained by the reader. Do I believe the current generation is beyond hope, not beyond, but certainly requiring a significant amount of time in the shop, through very little fault of their own I might ad. We are all a product of our times.

This labor of love began a little more than twenty years ago. I was the president of a small college in northern Minnesota and taking advantage of a perk in a system that allows a sabbatical leave of absence for those who qualify. I happened to be one of the fortunate ones. My graduate degrees were in education leadership and business administration. Therefore, I submitted a proposal to study leadership at both the educational and corporate levels. Specifically, leadership traits that defined and contributed to the overall success of a leader both positionally, and ultimately, in salary and/or prestige.

After my sabbatical leave was approved, there was a supervisory position change and the individual who had previously approved of my proposal had been replaced. The new administrator required there be tangible evidence of the efforts put forth during a sabbatical leave. My first book, *This Book Is No Joke!* is the compilation of these efforts.

Reflecting on these efforts, I discovered the number one trait of a successful leader, as well as the number one trait desired in a spouse, was the same; a sense of humor. Not to be confused with jokes or comedy, a true sense of humor is a disposition. The origin of this disposition is found in its name dating back centuries. According to Wilfred Funk, the author of *Word Origins and Their Romantic Stories,* we borrowed the term humor from the Latin, and in the mother language humor meant a liquid. The mixture (Latin: mixture=tempermentum) of bodily fluids would be an indication of one's health i.e., a humorous disposition.

I went on to identify the function of humor in communication, and the role it plays in diffusing conflict with countless examples from master communicators throughout history. Examples were cited from captains of industry, leading political figures, world leaders and quotes from scripture in order to illustrate the significance of humor in communication.

The question of where humor comes from, what happens to it, and how one can regain it is the focus of Part III in this book. In addition, research was conducted demonstrating that most people have an inflated sense of their own humor, evidenced by their subordinate evaluations. And rarely, will one admit to an absence of a sense of humor. A sense of humor is viewed as critical to our self-esteem and wellbeing.

The research findings compiled in book form (This Book Is No Joke!) were sufficient to justify a year's absence from campus. The presentation of the research results at the International Platform Association convention in Washington D.C. proved to be award winning.

Prior to my academic experience, I owned my own business in Australia and upon returning to the states worked as a probation counselor for the prosecutor's office in Kalamazoo, Michigan. I also began teaching theories of juvenile delinquency at a local community college and other courses in the field of criminal justice. I then accepted a faculty position with the department of criminal justice at Northern Michigan University (NMU) in Marquette, Michigan. While at NMU I began a criminal justice association that exposed students to casino security techniques in Las Vegas, Nevada in anticipation that native Americans were going to seek approval for casinos on reservation properties throughout the United States.

I continued my personal educational efforts simultaneously with my academic appointment with Northern Michigan University. I completed my doctorate (Ed.D.) in education leadership at Western Michigan University in Kalamazoo, Michigan. This effort included a sabbatical leave to The University of Las Vegas, Nevada (UNLV) to study the interpretation of Rorschach personality test. I also completed an internship with the homicide bureau in Detroit, Michigan. My doctorial dissertation was completed while assigned to the parole board of Michigan State. It was a study examining the rate of recidivism of inmates completing college associate degrees while incarcerated. Recidivism rates of this cohort were compared to released inmates who did not acquire a degree while incarcerated. This involved the cooperation of Jackson State Prison in Jackson, Michigan, which at the time, housed 6,000 inmates.

After a brief appointment with The University of Maine I made an abrupt jump from the academic world in Michigan due to an unanticipated opportunity and became the CEO of a professional medical billing service in Presque Isle, Maine. I was subsequently promoted to the position of CEO of the medical foundation sponsoring the billing service.

I soon realized I missed the research and teaching component of higher education and accepted an administrative appointment (Vice

Provost) at Northland Community College in northern Minnesota. I was promoted to Provost and then President of the college. I completed a master's in business administration (MBA) at St. Thomas University in St. Paul, Minnesota and subsequently, accepted the position of Senior Fellow for Academic Affairs for the thirty-four colleges in the Minnesota State System. This required me to relocate to St. Paul, Minnesota. In this position I coordinated a leadership program sponsored by the Kellogg Foundation that gained national recognition.

My next career move involved a jump from the academic world to the corporate world. I assumed the position as senior consultant for a sales training organization, Corporate Visions Inc. (CVI) located in Lake Tahoe, Nevada. This required international travel and training resulting in just under two million frequent flyer miles, equivalent to eighty-three trips around the world. I held this position for over a decade. Following this appointment, I became an independent consultant specializing in the area of corporate engagement.

I offer this mini-review of my work experience to convey an overview of my background demonstrating a variety of work environments not only in the United States, but worldwide. I have always been fascinated with what makes certain individuals so much more successful than others. Fortunately, I have had the opportunity in both educational and work environments to pursue the answer to that question. Ironically, I am equally intrigued with the opposite end of the social spectrum, and that is, what makes other people so vulnerable and prone to actions that will nearly guarantee that life will be a series of bad decisions? My education and experience in the field of criminal justice allowed me to gather firsthand knowledge of those volitions or choices that people make that will continue to make them prisoners of yesterdays' decisions.

To the individual experiencing the freedom of society, the concept of prison is a formidable thought. However, research indicates, some inmates become so adaptable they prefer incarceration to the freedom afforded to a law-abiding citizen. "Three snacks and a rack," is an expression of betterment among inmates working for eighteen cents an hour in the laundry room in exchange for free meals, accommodations, vision, dental and health insurance. Throw in some free concerts and cable television, and it's not too shabby of an existence. The only thing missing is some silence every now and then.

Ironically, a considerable number of citizens in free society are unaware they are falling victim to the same influences. By constantly becoming recipients of benefits that are unearned they also are forming psychological dependencies and life on the "outside" becomes a form of "self-imprisonment." This is why the importance of "self-esteem" and its reliance on positive critical decisions and behaviors are emphasized so heavily in this publication. The "On My Way" project which follows the epilogue focuses on the importance and development of self-esteem in children. This project is currently offered in public and parochial schools in Minnesota.

I feel privileged to have the opportunity to share these findings with the reader. With all the diverse cultures, personalities, and political differences along the spectrum of life, one issue remains critical as to which extreme is realized; one's ability to communicate effectively.

When I first addressed the problem back in 2001, I approached it from a positive posture seeking to identify the most desirable trait in effective communication. I now realize, along with the rest of the world, there is a far greater problem than poor communication and that is, no communication. In the first edition of *Bridging the Communication Gap,* released in 2015, I addressed what I had experienced around the world as proven communication techniques, in addition to the most desirable trait, i.e. sense of humor. These techniques are included in **The Last Book …** and include; critical choices, emotional tones, change avoidance, the influence of technology, and the concept of 'FLOW'.

The first Edition of Bridging the Communication Gap released in 2015, foreshadowed the events that were about to take place. It's not essential to pinpoint precisely when our national disposition began to change from a nation of one, to a nation of self-obsessed individuals. There are a variety of publications that address this social phenomenon, notably; *The Narcissism Epidemic by Twenge & Campbell,* with a cover tag line, "Chronicles the obsession that many Americans have with, well themselves…thinking themselves entitled to things they haven't earned." Also, notable; *Selfie, How We Became So Self-Obsessed and What It's Doing to Us by Will Storr.*

Most people are quick to acknowledge that narcissism, an inflated view of the self, is ubiquitous. For those in their teens and younger this is not a new phenomenon. They have entered this world with this dynamic of heighted individualism on full display. It's interesting to note in an audience with a wide range of ages, the youngest have difficulty recognizing, identifying, or acknowledging a cultural shift emphasizing "self" has occurred. However, the individuals more advanced in age are unanimous in their recognition that such a cultural movement has taken place.

If is very difficult to precisely pinpoint when a cultural shift takes place. It may be a defining moment like the Woodstock concert (1969), that suggest precision dating, or the introduction of the cellphone ('80) or smartphone ('02). For most cultural shifts the timing is vague.

I recently had a discussion with a colleague and suggested it was challenging for any adult over forty to perceive one as intelligent who sprinkles the acronym for "For Unlawful Carnal Knowledge" (more commonly referred to as the F-bomb) throughout their speech. He was amazed that middle-aged people would be offended by the usage of that word. Most people under forty years of age have grown up with the common use of this word. The movie Scarface ('83) drops 208 F-bombs, and Colors ('88) drops 157. If one is a member of the generation where the cultural change takes place it is barely noticeable.

"I first became aware of it one day on the subway," is offered by a conferee. "A young man stepped on the subway holding this huge box on his shoulder blasting out what I assumed to be music that was almost deafening to the rest of the passengers. My fellow passengers quickly made eye-exchanges, as if to convey disbelief of the audacious behavior. To this day I wonder, what made him believe that his individual needs were so superior to the rest of us?"

Other attendees were quick to offer their individual epiphanies as to when they realized there had been an alteration to the cultural norms. For one it was when she saw a bumper sticker, "I Love Me." For another, it was when she read about a woman who changed her 2-year-old son's name from Kevin to Kelvin to match the misspelled tattoo of his name on her arm. Another shared the accounting of a 31-year-old Florida woman who sent more than 65,000 text messages to a man with whom she had just one date. One of my favorites is advice offered by an Australian "sexuality educator" that parents should ask their baby's permission before changing diapers. She goes on to explain, "just by asking the parents are letting that child know that their response matters." I now realize my mom owes me some apologies!

One of my "aha" moments that something in the culture had changed was during the late seventies. It was in the movie, *Saturday Night Fever* (1977), and John Travolta was painstaking grooming his hair and fastidiously tucking his silk shirt in preparation for his night on the town. Later, watching his "all about me" entrance to the discotheque and his subsequent line-dance that mesmerized the standing-room only audience, it occurred to me what was missing in his preparation for the event. What was different from what I would experience, was any thought or involvement of his girl or date for the evening. It was as if she didn't exist in order for him to have this fulfilling evening.

Another reflection for me that times were changing was the celebrity that Joe Namath received during his football career with Alabama and later with the New York Jets. His white fur coat gleaned as much attention as the game and his famously quoted line, "I can't wait for tomorrow, because I get better looking every day," lives on. And times have changed.

My contribution to this psychological development was a workshop entitled; *Therapy on a Stick.* The primary premise of this seminar is the belief that society has created a toxic environment for our youth by perpetuating an illusion "to strive for social perfectionism." The unfortunate part is the definition of perfection is defined by social media and constantly changing. This uncertainty creates a variety of repercussions ranging from anxiety, depression, addiction, body image distortion, isolation and unfortunately, more than 45,000 suicides annually. Each of these deaths have their own circumstances. However, the lack of support and communication with stable support systems that were readily available in the past, including friends, neighbors, community organizations and relatives living nearby, now resides, "in-the-cloud." The pillars of support that were once readily available for communication remain available, however only at their convenience.

Is this period of self-obsession only temporary? One may hope so. However, it has proven to be resilient as it approaches its fiftieth-anniversary, with no sign of letting up thanks to social media.

Given the elements of The Perfect Storm as outlined in Part I of The Last Book ... the dynamics of leadership have been turned upside down. Those techniques and theories of leadership that have been groomed and survived the test of time are no longer relevant due to the fact the their application was based on a clearly defined chain of command. A chain that had specific roles and responsibilities with a clear distinction between leaders and followers. That chain has clearly been broken as illustrated in Part I of The Last Book ... The followers have disappeared!

Sections 1 thru 12 will focus on strategies and techniques that will enable individuals who still operate in the capacity of 'leaders' to survive in this land of no followers. Sections 13 thru 19 will provide a ray of light and hope by illuminating the most essential trait that will contribute to successful communication in these challenging times; a sense of humor. Not to be confused with jokes or comedy, but with a sense of openness and receptiveness to others and their ideas. This is the focus of Part III of The Last Book.....

Forgive me if I indulge in some historical references in order to emphasize the importance of this 'sense of humor' as it relates to effective communication. The use of historical personalities as examples will be better understood once the reader has had an opportunity to read the section on the perfect storm and the significance of partisanship. One contemporary example may cause some readers to go into a tailspin. Hopefully, this is not the case with the historical examples cited.

In the early stages of theory development relating to the importance of humor, the tenure of President Ronald Reagan was heaven sent. On a routine bases, frequently evident on the nightly news, one could witness the power and the essence of this sixth sense as President Reagan would further his agenda, and neutralize his opposition. This power to communicate effectively was not diminished by adversity or political opposition, and at the conclusion of his term he left office with the unofficial title, The Great Communicator.

Once the trait of humor was identified, and an awareness activated to record evidence of its use in order to facilitate effective communication there were ample historical examples readily available. Thus, the identity of the critical trait was revealed, however a more esoteric line of questioning emerged. Recognizing a highly developed sense of humor as a critical factor to one's success, what was its origin, and more importantly, what happens to it? Both of these issues are discussed at some length in the book. Therefore, with the trait, its origin, and its demise within the individual identified, what is the reluctance to bring the issue to a close at this time? Enter Governor Jessie Ventura.

Just as Ronald Reagan was heaven sent in revealing the importance of a sense of humor, Governor Jessie Ventura was heaven sent in reference to examining the issue of what happens to one's sense of humor. The reader may recognize the stated theory that one's sense of humor, and the prerequisites of spontaneity and curiosity, are slowly eroded in the individual by virtue of the influences of parents, peers, and the socialization process. The "press" becomes one of these socialization pressures that attempt to transform the individual. And frequently, with great success. The political pressure applied to Governor Jessie Ventura during his first year in office is the quintessential "case in point."

Much to the surprise of the State, Nation, and the World, Jessie "the body" Ventura was elected as the nation's first Reform Party governor of the State of Minnesota in November 1998. His platform, posture, and presentation were nothing short of refreshing to those Minnesotans' who were tired of the predictability of the two party system, fierce partisanship, ideological extremism and indifference to disaffected voters.

In his first year of office, Minnesota's 38th governor is frequently credited with being a key player in the $2.9 billion sales tax rebate, permanent income tax rate reduction, a light-rail package, additional education funding, health endowments with the tobacco windfall, and a successful trade mission to Japan. A commendable effort for 12-months of work.

James G. Janos, aka Jessie Ventura has always been very open about his style and motivation for seeking the governorship. In his autobiography, "I Ain't Got Time to Bleed," Jessie expresses his willingness to accept a challenge. "I love a challenge. I love living life to the fullest. I've worked hard for everything I've achieved. I've taken risks along the way, and I have few regrets." He openly admits to his nonconforming nature. "There's some kind of bachelor strain running through my dad's side of the family; an independent streak, a taste for not having to answer to anybody."

Let's take a look at that desire to "not having to answer to anybody." As a result of a whimsical comment made on the David Letterman show attributing the complex street design of St. Paul to someone drunk . . . "I think it was those Irish guys." A November '99 interview with Playboy magazine has proven to be most controversial, as playful comments are given literary scrutiny far beyond what the readership is accustomed. Do the governor's critics really believe he wants to come back as a 38-DD bra, or do they want to mold Jessie into something that conforms more responses reflective of "politics as usual?"

While George F. Will of the Washington Post headlines that, "Spontaneity helps make Ventura into a leading cultural indicator," Will presses the point on ABC-TV's "This week with Sam Donaldson and Cokie Roberts" with reference to the 38-DD comment, suggest that governor Ventura has a certain obligation to worry about the country's sense of dignity." To which Ventura appropriately responded, "Oh come on. Have we gotten to the point, George [that] I have to get elected and lose my sense of humor?"

The pressure for Jessie to become someone other than who he is, is mounted. The public is insistent that he be less spontaneous in his remarks. Try to evaluate what this degree of intensity of pressure does to enhance conforming, predictable behavior and subsequently what it does to one's sense of humor. In response to Jessie's spontaneous remarks a commentary from Jessie's hometown newspaper the Star Tribune (Oct.6,'99), has headlined, "Gov.Ventura should apologize or pack his bags." A new line of T-shirts with the following slogans are now available, "Pro Wrestling Is a Sham and a Crutch for Weak-Minded People" and "Our Governor Can Fit More Feet in His Mouth Than Your Governor." And a former Ventura ally is the first person ever to initiate a recall drive against a state officeholder. The home town newspaper also reports that according to a CNN/USA Today/Gallup poll of U.S. adults (973 respondents), favorable opinion of Ventura has dropped from 51% in September [prior to the Playboy article], to 37%. Those with an unfavorable view of the governor jumped from 25% to 45% during the same period.

He apologized to offended St. Paulites for the Irish remark, but added glumly, "We've somehow lost our sense of humor." In an October '99 interview with Newsweek magazine, the man who enjoys, "not having to answer to anybody," states, "You can be yourself and get elected, but you can't be yourself and govern." He went on, "You have to give the correct answers. You have to give the answers that don't offend anyone." And perhaps, most telling of the impact of the criticism of him during the first year, he states in the Newsweek interview, "I'm not going to offer my personal opinions on anything." He confesses, "In light of my family and self-preservation. I know that I have to change."

For Jessie the "risk taker" with "few regrets" certainly must have been reflecting on what is necessary in order to make the compromises required of his position as governor of the state of Minnesota. Contemplating if in fact, the position is worth the individual compromise. He has already rewritten the history books for the state of Minnesota, need he do more? What would a good navy seal do?

Every day, the pressures for Jessie to compromise and conform, and become someone other than who he was when elected, were enormous. Unfortunately, played out in front of a worldwide readership. An essential message in this book, is for all of us to be aware that a similar scenario was played out in our life. Perhaps not as public as that experienced by Jessie Ventura, but nevertheless as instrumental in our development. In our early, formative years, we made choices as to the degree we would compromise in order to "fit in." Those compromises, to our spontaneity, take a toll on our sense of humor as an adult.

Fortunately, Section 17 addresses the risks necessary to reverse the adverse effects of these lifelong compromises, and contribute to the return of this sixth sense, that has been repressed, and so critical to personal success.

The obvious question that remains pertaining to recaptureing one's sense of humor is, "If one recognizes the importance of this sixth sense, and the ease with which it can be recultivated, why are we so reluctant to do so? The most obvious answer is, and unfortunately so, who we are presently, even if not desirable, is a known quantity. And to change this known quantity, requires risk into the unknown. We like safe.

The late Psychologist, Abraham H. Maslow, former president of the American Psychological Association, offers some insight as to why we are willing to remain in our present form, even if undesired by us. He identifies this resistance as, The Jonah Complex. The same Jonah referred to in scripture, and taking temporary residence inside a whale. In his earlier notes, Maslow referred to these phenomena as the "fear of one's own greatness" or the "evasion of one's destiny" or the "running away from one's own best talents."

In scripture, The prophet Jonah is commanded by God to go to Nineveh, the wicked capital city of the Assyrians, to preach repentance. Instead, Jonah disobeys God and boards a ship to Tarshish in southern Spain. The ship encounters great storms. Jonah knows he is the cause of the storms and the crew agrees to Jonahs' request to be thrown overboard. Subsequently, Jonah is swallowed by a great fish, and three days later regurgitated on dry land and again commanded by God to go to Nineveh. This time Jonah goes and experiences resounding success.

According to Maslow, like Jonah, "we run away from the responsibilities dictated by nature, by fate, and even sometimes by accident, just as Jonah tried-in vain-to run away from his fate. It is certainly possible for most of us to be greater than we are in actuality. We have unused potentialities or not fully developed ones. It is certainly true that many of us evade our constitutionally suggested vocations (call, destiny, task in life, mission)."

We fear our highest possibilities. We are generally afraid to become that which we can glimpse in our most perfect moments, under the most perfect conditions, under conditions of greatest courage. We enjoy and even thrill to the godlike possibilities we see in ourselves as we employ the communication techniques cited in this edition including critical choices, emotional tones, change avoidance, the influence of technology, and the concept of FLOW in such peak moments." Enjoy these moments, one step at a time.

The trouble with life is, you are halfway through before you realize it is one of those 'do-it-yourself' deals.

-Unleash Your Greatness (Olson & Strand)

INTRODUCTION

I sincerely believe to be in the presence of one communicating effectively is comparable to listening to a beautiful piece of music, watching a priceless work of art unfold on a canvas, watching an artisan complete a clay molding or a glass blower completing his work of art with a precise flick of the wrist. To watch one flow from pleasant conversation with the neighbor, to light exchanges with the bag boy at the grocery store, to colleagues at work, with supervisors and subordinates, to loved ones at home is nothing short of watching a royal ballet being performed at center stage. It is beauty to behold.

This ability to communicate like a master craftsman does not come naturally. It takes years of varied experiences and a multitude of situations to learn the craft. It requires the flexibility of a journeyman and the strength of a gladiator to hold firm and defend a position you know is right. It requires the empathy of a nun and the magic of a firefly to abruptly change luminescence when another person enters the room.

Unfortunately, if one were forced to reveal the name of one who possessed this quality to communicate effectively, one most likely would reach for the history books and produce one of few that come to mind: Gandhi, Thoreau, or possibly Christ. Dale Carnegie ran into this problem nearly one hundred years ago when the University of Chicago and the United Y.M.C.A. Schools conducted a survey to determine what adults want to study. The survey revealed that health is the prime interest of adults, and their second interest is people: how to understand and get along with people, how to make people like you, and how to win others to your way of thinking.

A leading capitalist at the time, John D. Rockefeller echoed the same by stating, "The ability to deal with people is as purchasable a commodity as sugar or coffee. And I will pay more for that ability than for any other under the sun."

At this time the search was on to find the textbook that would accompany the critical course. According to Dale Carnegie, the end result was the confession, "I know what those adults want. But the book they need has never been written." Carnegie began the class, starting with a set of rules printed on a card no larger than a postcard. The next season they printed a larger card, then a leaflet, than a series of booklets, and after fifteen years of experiment and research came the book, *How to Win Friends & Influence People*. Eighty years later; the concern remains and the resources are still lacking.

Bridging the Communication Gap attempts to fill in some of the potholes that have accumulated during those eighty years while recognizing some of the aspirations of the current reader. For openers, the earlier concerns discovered by the Y.M.C.A. are as relevant today as they were eighty years ago. Many would argue the communication, or lack thereof, problem has become worse, and there are several reasons for this. We have lived through an age of tremendous growth including the innovation of the pill, electronics, computers, and the birth of the internet. In addition, we have television, antibiotics, space travel, civil rights, feminism, teenagers, the green revolution, gay rights, high speed trains and cars, and walking on the moon. All are relevant and exciting accomplishments, and discussions relating to effective communication pale alongside these advancements.

Many of the technological advancements have impinged on our ability to communicate, and they are more engaging than just "talking." This common concurrence makes it acceptable for all members of the family to indulge in modern media while out to dinner. In the old days, it might just be dad who would disengage and read the paper while others conversed. The limitation on the number of characters in addition to the expectation of an immediate response has limited our patience and our attention span to that of a hummingbird. To suggest a "family discussion" over any given issue is tantamount to a suicide pact.

I notice the latest communication technique that seems to be in vogue is to just increase your volume if you want your opinion known and/or to talk over the person who is offering an opposing view. This technique seems to be gaining momentum on a daily basis.

I don't begrudge any of the advances, just the acknowledgement that referencing back to a problem (communication) that has existed well over one hundred years is not nearly as interesting as talking about the latest release from Apple. Which is more appealing, talking about the new 50" flat screen to be placed on the den wall or the septic tank system that must be replaced? No doubt the flat screen will be up, and the septic will continue to fester.

In any event, this book is written with the contemporary reader in mind. It spares the reader of undue research by providing an ample listing of resources in the back of the book. It has one very clear and simple purpose, and that is to allow the reader to challenge the author regarding the techniques suggested. Each of the concepts is presented with the intent that it will make the reader more aware and at the same time more assertive in becoming an effective communicator. It is anticipated and expected that the reader will apply the concept immediately.

The book deals with communication, more specifically, with the lack thereof in contemporary society. More importantly, it addresses how an individual may communicate more effectively by merging a few concepts, presented in a simplistic fashion without undue time and resources committed to theoretical explanations and academic arguments. In short, these techniques work and this is why.

In Part I the four ingredients of the perfect storm were identified; partisanship, narcissism, technology and litigation. Combined they serve to halt communication, and leave "leader's" without a following. The balance of the book will focus on those skills and techniques which will enable those serving in a leadership capacity to be effective.

Part II begins with an overview of the role of engagement in the contemporary workplace. I focus on this because I believe the word "engagement" is the "twenty-first century in-word" in the business lexicon. Like the word "motivation," I believe the term "engagement" will have an active shelf-life that approaches 100 years. It will be used indiscriminately by consultants like me to justify outrageous fees, and reserve the right to define it as the situation requires. According to Maylett and Warner, organizations currently spend about $720 million a year in the United States alone on programs intended to increase employee engagement. And that figure is expected to double.

This section will focus on the key drivers as well as the benefits of engagement to an organization. It will emphasize the role of the supervisor as it relates to engagement and how to communicate effectively in order to enhance engagement. The key roadblocks to engagement will be introduced, and the most popular escape routes that make the exchange of information more difficult will be revealed.

In Section 2, we will examine the role of communication as it relates to the ability to develop relationships and the perceived value of this ability as it relates to success and income in the real world. It answers the question, "How can one person be so much more valuable than another to an organization?"

In Section 3, I begin to drift down the path of self-indulgence. As a lifelong educator in the classroom or the boardroom, as well as a former college president, I have always been fascinated by the lack of communication that takes place within the "ivory tower" of higher education. This section of reflection will clarify to the reader why it is the faculty members don't like the students, the administration, or the institution. Yes, it has to do with communication. However, I felt compelled to include this chapter, since the book is written from the perspective of a college classroom. This setting was ideal to communicate the relevant concerns of bridging the communication gap in a creative nonfiction format.

Section 4 takes us down another slippery slope as we examine the critical traits of leadership in an attempt to isolate the most critical trait of all. Section 5 identifies this critical trait and expands its origins, its demise, and the necessary steps to take to revive it.

In Section 6, we examine the steps necessary to achieve high self-esteem and in Section 7 the choices one must make on a daily and even an hourly bases to assure a high level of self-esteem.

Assuming people are able to exercise the appropriate choices in order to achieve high self-esteem, how do they recognize and choose the people of a like quality in order to assure effective communication takes place? This becomes the focus of Section 8.

Once people reach this pinnacle of achievement, exercising full and effective communication to assure personal and professional success, how do they continue to be challenged? This question becomes the focus of Section 9.

Given the blueprint of success in Sections I through 9, why would anyone refuse to become fully engaged in becoming all they can be? Enter Section 10, which examines why it is that people refuse to make the necessary changes in lifestyle in order to become fully actualized.

Section 11 provides an isolated example of the power of resistance that exist within all of us to withstand the influence of outside forces and opinions to modify an established behavior, even if it is for our own betterment.

Section 12, concludes by drawing the reader's attention to the influence that technology has had on communication over the past fifty years. In summary, we have grown lazy in our efforts to innovate new technologies since our roller coaster ride in the "Golden Quarter" (1945 to 1971). We have improved our technologies, but for the most part they are not "new" or "innovative" technologies. But nowhere is our laziness more apparent than our inability to communicate with one another. We have been lulled to sleep in the most important aspect of our lives as we attempt to relate to those we work with, live next to, and love the most.

Part III will focus on perhaps the most critical trait required of those assuming leadership responsibilities in the twenty-first century; the ability to diffuse conflict. This is the trait that the corporate world considers 'priceless'. The ability to move independent people and projects forward as a united body of effort while existing in a perfect storm. The quest to discover this trait began twenty-five years ago when the author took a sabbatical leave to pursue the question, What makes an individual worth $8,653.85 an hour? This was the widely publicized salary of Lee Iacocca by the Chrysler Corporation at the time. This research to find the answer to that question led to the publication of the book; *This Book Is No Joke!* These findings are contained in ***The Last Book ...***

Part IV of the book will describe the ***On My Way Project, (On My Way to Becoming the Person I was meant to be).*** This is a project that caters to elementary school students in their efforts to build positive self-esteem. It is based on research that identifies the most common regrets that senior citizens have and addressing those issues while young, thus avoiding the regrets later in life. In the process of addressing the regrets, the students will be enhancing their own self-esteem at an early age.

PART I

THE PERFECT STORM

PARTISANSHIP

―◆✕◆―

At the beginning of The Last Book… I purposedly avoided any examples of issues that would possibly be considered partisan issues in an effort to avoid "poking the bear," and losing possible readers. The entire issue of partisanship was introduced to accentuate it's significant role in creating "The Perfect Storm." Partisanship was joined with narcissism, technology and litigation to form the most perfect of storms. And the balance of the book was to isolate a specific trait or disposition that is essential in dealing with this perfect storm. This trait was a sense of humor in it's purest form which is a disposition of openness and receptivity to others and their respective views. The importance of this type of individual to an organization is priceless.

Precisely when the intense partisan division that we experience today began is difficult to identify. However, we know some of the issues that encouraged its maturation and subsequent influence on the budding relative that gained prominence in the 70's; narcissism. Certainly, the Vietnam war had a tremendous impact and divisive influence on the country and encouraged the declaration of separation and positioning regarding the war. And rightfully so, it was a matter of life or death for those eligible to participate. This affected established coalitions like unions, farmers, religious affiliations, teachers and both blue and white collared workers. This one issue forced citizens to choose a camp, and thus, the maturation of partisanship.

Once the camps were established, and the stakes were planted, it was just a matter of selecting an issue. It became issues with no boundaries. Today it transcends the "preferred lexicon" to the establishment of the Alumni Free Speech Alliance now existing at MIT, Stanford, Princeton, UVA and others. These students and faculty are uniting to fight back against what they perceive to be a partisan culture and enjoy a culture of free speech.

Given that the reader has stuck with it for some eighteen sections I am empowered to push forward with a great deal of bravado to identify and lay bare some of the obstacles that may be a hindrance to the reader in achieving this desired state or disposition.

Earlier I referenced the tremendous influence my father was on me, and the respect he had for the work of Dale Carnegie as it relates to effective communications and human relations. I remember one of the time-tested adages was to avoid conversations relating to politics, religion or money. That has proven to be good advice; however the list has grown considerably longer thanks to the prejudices inherent in partisan politics and the obsession that many Americans have with themselves. That obsession, commonly referred to as narcissism, will be revisited next in the aftermath.

The reader is challenged to suspend any biases or prejudices that may exist in order to receive maximum benefit from this next exercise. In preparation to defend much of the content contained within this book I thought I would expand on my father's earlier advise to avoid the big three; politics, religion or money. I would ask the reader to go down this expanded (not to be considered exhausted) listing of randomly selected "Top Twenty Topics" and ask the question: Am I capable of addressing each of these topics in a calm, intelligent manner that will result in some form of resolution without turning into a raging person and making all sort of value judgements about the person with an opposing view? I have omitted the inclusion of any specific person or country in order to negate any possible melt downs, just issues.

Partisan Issues Sampler

- Abortion
- Automatic Weapons
- Black Lives Matter
- Boarder Issues
- Climate Concerns
- Critical Race Theory (CRT)
- Crime
- Diversity
- Entitlements
- Gender Identity
- Homelessness
- Inflation
- Leash Laws
- Mandatory National Service
- Political Affiliation
- Reparations
- Social Media Influence
- Supreme Court Configuration
- Term Limits
- Tuition Refunds

Just to name a few…

Now imagine how the conversation would flow with two individuals who both possessed the trait of humor as they addressed the "Top Twenty". Bearing in mind that humor has nothing to do with jokes or comedy, but does reflect a disposition of openness and respect for others and their opinions.

Ironically, many of the above twenty topics are not new, they have been around for years which begs the question; Why hasn't something been done? John Kotter in his book, *The Heart of Change* insist that first of all, one must create a sense of urgency among relevant people, and secondly one must be aware of four common causes for this lack of progress.

Four sets of behaviors commonly stop the launch of needed change:

1. Complacency, driven by false pride or arrogance.
2. Immobilization, driven by fear or panic.
3. Deviance, driven by anger.
4. Hesitation, driven by a pessimistic attitude.

The reason individuals possessing a sense of humor can remain objective is that their self-esteem does not rest on a need to be right. Part of what makes this proposed dialogue of the "Top Twenty" so stressful is the entrenched partisan view that one's beliefs or position is the correct one. This entrenched view of one's opinion lies at the feet of our second climate factor: narcissism.

NARCISSISM

Narcissism is the fuel that feeds partisanship. It intensifies the response forcing the fuel into a combustion chamber that does not allow compromise. The history of narcissism reflex's a complex phenomenon. Ironically, it begins with efforts to elevate self-esteem by normalizing efforts. Elevating those individuals that were not that exceptional, to immediately have inflated opinions of themselves. Therefore, awards to identify excellence (MVP), were eliminated. However, awards that recognized participation were encouraged. Honor rolls were eliminated to avoid making others feel inferior and, in many instances, grades were eliminated completely. The expression of, "All boats rise together" ruled the day. Recently, college entrance exams have been eliminated at major colleges to enhance the inclusion of all candidates.

In addition to blatant efforts to increase self-worth many theories of self-development emerged that suggested the attainment of self-worth was within the grasp of everyone. This would include Maslow's Hierarchy of Needs and Brandon's The Psychology of Self-Esteem. The arts encouraged self-expression and dual incomes required parental supervision to be at a minimum thus creating a self-survival confidence that had not existed before. Parental guilt due to absence curtailed previous efforts to discipline and were frequently substituted with monetary awards. In 1971, narcissistic personality disorder (NPD) was identified and in 1980 was officially included in the DSM-III, the handbook of psychiatric disorders.

Narcissism has had an interesting history since its inception in the 1970's and official recognition as a diagnosable disorder in 1980. Interesting in the sense that there would be strong support from a segment of the population that may have seen tremendous growth in some individuals, and tragic results in others. The support would come from parents, peers, siblings and possibly school personnel who have watched the 'rose burst from the bud'. As adults it may be evident in promotions at work, recognition in the community and a significant elevation in self-worth in the individual.

The lack of support for the narcissistic individual may come from another contingency equal in number and superior in venom as a result of their association with the narcissistic personality. The venom may be directed toward the anxiety, depression, eating disorders, and suicide attempts they have witnessed. The complete disruption of a family due to unrestricted selfishness and self-indulgence on the part of the narcissistic individual is not uncommon.

Unfortunately, this self-rightness indignation of the narcissistic personality is not only instrumental in the formation of the perfect storm, but instrumental in the obstruction of productive communication. They become the immovable object in an attempt to move the dialog forward. And unfortunately, there is little evidence this will change in the foreseeable future. All the more reason to have one knowledgeable in communication techniques at the helm to respond. This is you, and your knowledge of the need to be open and receptive to this individual who is not capable of such flexibility.

Over the years as I have witnessed the acceptance and proliferation of the narcissistic personality in our society. I have witnessed a unique approach and frequently very effective end result in negotiating with this personality type. But first, a quick clarification relating to this personality trait is in order. Be reminded that this trait became exceedingly popular beginning in the 1970's, some fifty years ago. Therefore, for individuals under fifty years of age this trait of narcissism is not unusual at all. It is considered the norm. This reality was pointed out earlier when I mentioned individuals who casually drop the

"F-bomb" in conversation are totally unaware of how offensive this might be to their elders. And I'm sure to break out a phone and take a "selfie" and post it immediately with no shame or guilt regardless of the audience is totally acceptable to the more youthful population. Also be reminded that this elevated opinion of one's self, and one's opinion is what creates the inflexibility within the narcissistic as they defend their partisan beliefs.

However, there is hope. And once again the hope lies within the individual who possess the openness and receptiveness to another's point of view, the individual who has the sense of humor. As mentioned, there are several techniques addressing this preconceived resistance of the narcissistic personality. The first is to never say "No" directly to a narcissist. This will armor them to fight to the death whatever the issue may be. A much more effective response would be; "I hear what your saying," You make a good point," That's an interesting observation," "I've never looked at it that way before," "When you put it that way, I see light at the end of the tunnel." You get the idea, a constant positive endorsement or encouragement of exchange. This sounds easy enough, however if you are under fifty years of age you may feel some discomfort in this self-denying exchange. One can only speculate as to how many of the "Top Twenty" may have been resolved years ago with this approach.

The inflexible narcissist may best be understood by examining his parallel the Echoist. The echoist is the counterpart to the narcissistic. As Donna Christina Savery a psychotherapist in London documents in her book; *Echoism: The Silenced Response to Narcissism,* echoism is a distinct clinical phenomenon adapting themselves to the perceived wishes of others. As the name implies, they lack their own voice. Unlike the narcissist, they have a strong aversion to attention, with a fear of seeming narcissistic in any way. They are so compatible to the narcissist because it is a relief to be with someone who relishes taking up all the space.

According to Craig Malkin, PH.D., a clinical psychologist at Harvard Medical School and cited in *Psychology Today*, echoists can be terrific listeners, but their ability to share is limited (as the name implies). They bury their needs in the hope that they'll be accepted and loved for demanding so little. They see this trait as a survival strategy by seeing themselves as a burden and blaming themselves for being sensitive, needy, or high maintenance. They rarely feel special, therefore their dread of feeling special, appears to be a significant problem as the narcissist's addiction to it. They live at opposite ends of the self-enhancement spectrum and yet seem to complement each other.

The origin of Echo and Narcissus dates back to Ovid (43 BC), a Roman poet who lived during the reign of Augustus. Ovid had a tremendous influence on countless authors, poets and playwrights including Shakespeare. Echo and Narcissus is a myth from Ovid's Metamorphoses, a Roman mythological epic. Echo is a mountain nymph who is rejected by Narcissus when he falls in love with his own reflection. Echo is invisible and can only repeat words that other's have already spoken. It is a parable with a central theme that teaches one to be aware of the trap of vanity or self-adoration. This is a theme or caution that has landed on deaf hears in the most recent half century. There is a lesson to be learned here.

This self-aggrandized disposition of a true narcissist is what contributes to the immobilization of progress (It's all about me), as well as being identified as one of the components of the perfect storm at the beginning of **The Last Book...** A fact that on the surface can be somewhat demoralizing. However, I do think there iis evidence of a rainbow even in this situation. We can assume in an effort to work with this unique personality type, the narcissist, there are some expressions that may be incorporated ("I hear what you're saying") that will have a ring of compromise to them. In addition, we must take note that everyone is not necessarily an enemy to the narcissist. The echoist among us has found a way to win them over by constantly compromising and putting themselves last in order to maintain harmony.

In order to understand this dynamic of communication, we must flash back to Section 8, Ruth Minshull's, *How to Choose Your People*. In her book she reserves a special chapter for the type of person who fits the echo mode, and how they interact with the narcissistic type of individual. She calls that particular tone, 'Propitiation.' Webster defines propitiation: To appease and make favorable; . friendly overtures to gain someone's favor. They give themselves, their services, their talent, their time, their possessions or their creations. They seem to ask for nothing in return. This tone is a paradox because it looks so admirable at first glance according to Minshull. Intention makes the difference. In the compulsive propitiatory person, the intention is to **stop.** How this translates to working with the narcissistic individual in the real world would be to offer something in exchange for what you truly want, and satisfy them with something that elevates their opinion of themselves.

Minshull's book was written during the birth of the narcissistic movement; 1972, and I couldn't help but notice two other books on the shelve next to hers. Both best sellers and written during the glory days of the narcistic movement. Their titles say it all; Looking Out for #1 (1977), and Winning Through Intimidation (1973), both by Robert J. Ringer. This book, his first, was rejected 23 times and he decided to self-publish. It became a #1 New York Times Best Seller spending 36 weeks at the top.

His next book has a title that compliments the theme of ***The Last Book ...*** and that is *Restoring the American Dream (1979).* This book reached #3 on the New York Times Bestseller listings and was published by a company established by Ringer, Stratford Press. Ringer addresses the partisan divide over social issues and states. "There are no such things as 'social problems'; only individuals have problems, and since each individual's circumstances are unique, so too are his problems."

Ringer reserves his most poignant comments for the government, and will be addressed in the upcoming litigation section. In conclusion of this section focusing on the narcissistic personality, and their insistence they alone can provide the solution to any partisan issue that may arise, we move on to the influence of modern technology as it relates to the perfect storm.

TECHNOLOGY

> We are crossing a technology threshold that will forever change the way we learn, work, socialize and shop. It will affect all of us in ways far more pervasive than most people recognize.
>
> —Bill Gates

The reason that technology is such a vital component of the 'Perfect Storm' is it allows immediate access and support to **any** idea or position held. Please note, I did not include the adjective **rational** prior to the word idea, because that is not a perquisite for the acceptance or rejection for any idea, no matter how outrageous. Therein lies the problem. This immediate endorsement is what gives any idea legs and also a false impression of significance. In the past, prior to the advent of the web, an idea would be debated, perhaps picked up by the press, and magazines would follow with reaction later in the month. With limited time available on the nightly news broadcast there may be a brief mention of a concern, however very difficult to get momentum or endorsement with such limited exposure. That dynamic of limited exposure is no longer a consideration. Now the world knows the issue instantaneously and has an opinion simultaneously. Once again, this is what gives technology such a critical role in the formation of 'The Perfect Storm.'

For the youth of today it is difficult to realize how recent and rapidly this alternative in communication medium has occurred. To reach 50 million North America users, radio took 38 years and television took 13 years. The Internet reached 50 million people in 5 years. "The Internet speeds up everything to real-time simultaneously erodes time and distance, revives human communication on a planet-wide basis and puts everybody and everything immediately in touch," according to futurist Frank Feather in his book, future consumer.com.

Research is beginning to suggest a correlation between the heavy use of social media platforms and the Dark Triad; a cluster of personality traits that includes psychopathy, Machiavellianism, and narcissism. Social media have created a great environment for self-obsession to thrive.

Jesse Fox of Ohio State University published a study looking at whether the Dark Triad was a predictor of the amount of time men spent on the social networking sites and the number of selfies they posted. Her article is known for being the first academic study on selfies. She also established that all three Dark TrIad traits were correlated with the amount of time spent on social networking sites.

"We are very Pavlovian,"Fox says. "People get this jolt, this experience of approval and immediate validation every time they get a like or a viewer, and they cannot turn off that sense of reward." One of the reasons qualities such as entitlement, vanity, exploitative-ness and exhibitionism may be increasing is because the overarching personality type that is tied to them, narcissism, is not distressing or undesirable to those who possess it, according to journalist Mike Mariani.

Of course, the early victims of the perfect storm will be the book publishers. Potential readers, with strong partisan beliefs, will sit on the sidelines and not purchase books that have the slightest hint of opposition support. True narcissist will assume comprehensive knowledge of the issue at hand and see no reason to invest.

LITIGATION

Felipe Fernandez-Armesto pays tribute to the 'American Dream' in his book, *Ideas That Changed the World*. In his opening paragraph entitle; The Idea of American Exceptionalism, he states, "The idea that the United States is a unique country, beyond comparison with others, is older than the nation itself. It was part of the "pioneer spirit" – The shinning-faced enthusiasm that saw America as a promised land for chosen people. In the 19th century, some "different" expectations seemed fulfilled. The US became successively a model republic, an exemplary democracy, a burgeoning empire, a magnet for migrants, a precocious industrializer, and a great power. America, according to Americanism, could learn nothing from the rest of the world."

What a wonderful endorsement to this country and its' people. Unfortunately, the last sentence in this uplifting quotation is perhaps the most telling; we felt "we could learn nothing from the rest of the world." And as a result of this attitude, we have failed to learn from those great powers that have preexisted. It is difficult to pinpoint exactly when we began to lose our way. Some would say it was the Vietnam war when there may not have been a decisive defeat, and no conclusive victory. One thing was very evident, and that is young men were clearly not willing to volunteer to fight for the right to defend this model nation. It is no coincidence this attitude gained a substantial following at approximately the same time the "Me" generation was gaining momentum.

Some would indicate the tell-tale sign of our country's' decay was The Watergate scandal which stemmed from the President of the United States' legal team's persistent attempts to cover up it's involvement in the 1972 break-in of the Watergate Office Building. This cover-up led to the President's resignation.

In my estimation these incidents were all an indication that the wheels were beginning to fall off the wagon. I'm sure each generation will identify those incidents that resonate during their lifetime as being the critical factors that led to the demise of this nation. For example, my parents would identify the world wars, prohibition, and the subsequent depression as key contributing factors that have tarnished our reputation.

Unfortunately, we have something far more insidious at work and perhaps fatal for our culture. We don't have the fortitude or resilience that we once had that allowed us to focus on issues that would move us forward as a country. The combined forces of the perfect storm (partisanship, narcissism, technology and litigation), have allowed us to become more preoccupied with ourselves than focused on the critical issues at hand.

In addition, we have begun to weaponized our legal system in order to ease our burden and avoid addressing the critical issues. We are less interested in preserving our common rights than in exercising our individual rights. Change occurs in two primary ways: through trust and truth or through dissent and conflict. As the quality of leadership declines, the quantity of problems escalates. The confusion, ambiguity, and the complexity of the law tend toward paralysis, augmented by conflicting judicial interpretations. In the past, events and personalities were the focus of our discontent. Our legal system was considered sacrosanct. Precisely when that began to deteriorate is difficult to identify, as it intensifies with every election cycle and has never been more evident than the present.

Our legal system, and our entire system of justice have been compromised while we attend to ourselves. These systems make up the very soul of our nation and they are now in jeopardy. I could easily list the top twenty apparent breaches of injustice and then spend the next twenty pages allowing each side of the isle to defend their position by pointing out the transgressions of the opposition. If I did succumb, I would merely be echoing the past twenty years of debate. This book was written to point out the futility of that effort and recognize the need for individuals with enhanced communication skills to step forward and embrace how we are collectively able to create new realities.

PART II

COMMUNICATION IN THE 21ST CENTURY

PART I

SECTION 1

ENGAGEMENT

"*Why is it that we can get along with virtually any human being we come in contact with, with the exception of our immediate supervisor?*" It can be a complete stranger; it can be someone who has inadvertently called the wrong number, or someone we have been matched with through a number of dating services. All of these adventitious meetings will be more celebrated than the daily exchange we have with our supervisor.

More challenging may be an acceptable explanation as to why, immediately following our promotion, do we immediately become the lead leper in the colony? So begins the onslaught of questions accompanying a new set of graduate students and a new semester. A new semester that will review management theory and leadership proposals that have survived the scrutiny of time and will remain for decades to come. Let us begin with a contemporary term that has captured the imagination of many in the field of leadership theory: engagement.

One of the great chasms that exists in communication is the gap between employer and employee. More specifically, the gap between supervisor and employee is a critical concern that carries considerable impact if not resolved. This dynamic is frequently the deciding factor determining if one continues to pursue a career in a specific field or elects to move on to other challenges and opportunities. This gap has a huge influence on the home environment as a significant member of the household carries home a disposition strongly influenced by the communication or lack thereof that takes place between two employees on any given day. It is the plague that circulates among employees in the work environment but remains unmentioned until "disengagement" mentally or physically takes place.

Few terms in recent years have captured the imagination of the business community like the term, "engagement." Not since Abraham Maslow introduced his theory of Motivation Hierarchy in 1954 in his book, *Motivation and Personality,* have we embraced a concept so willingly and completely. Both engagement and motivation have similar appeal. They make very abstract concepts visually appealing to an intuitive mind. Therein lies their power and popularity.

My introduction to Maslow dates back to psychology classes in high school and college. The theory simply states that man has certain basic needs: food, water, and shelter to survive. These needs are expressed at

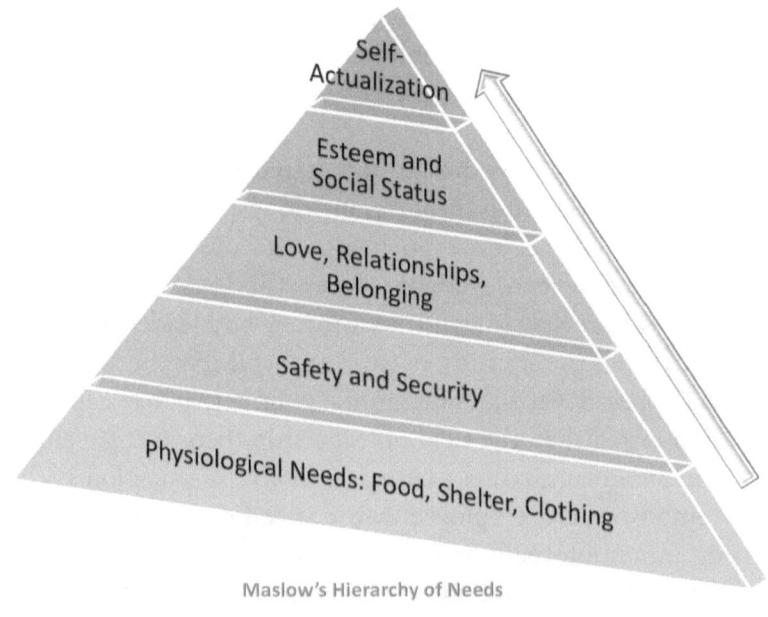

Maslow's Hierarchy of Needs

the base of an imaginary pyramid and once these needs are satisfied, an individual is motivated to seek the next higher level needs. This upward progression continues as long as the lower needs are met and ultimately culminates at the highest level, or in Maslow's terms, a self-actualized individual.

In spite of the popularity of Maslow's theory, I vividly recall one professor throwing Maslow under the bus by quoting a work which if memory serves me right was entitled; *Maslow Revisited*. According to this professor, Maslow's work reflected the results of a very small and inadequate sampling of individuals, and within that sampling there are few if any significant findings to indicate that individuals would progress up this hierarchy of needs once the lower needs were met and little evidence to indicate that all people desire these unique or specific needs. This argument would suggest there are many people who are quite content to stay at the lower levels of the pyramid, opposed to pursuing higher aspirations.

Recently, David Zweig has identified another very prominent grouping of workers who fail to conform to Maslow's hierarchy of progression. Zweig refers to these individuals and collectively as "Invisibles" in his recent book entitled *Invisibles: The Power of Anonymous Work in an Age of Relentless Self-Promotion (2014)*. According to Zweig, these hidden professionals (Invisibles) embody three traits: 1) Ambivalence toward recognition, 2) Meticulousness, and 3) Savoring of responsibility. The identification and acceptance of this cohort within the contemporary work environment may refute the earlier contribution by Maslow.

In any event, I was bummed out when I heard the criticism pertaining to Maslow's work because I had frequently resorted to this theory as a college instructor on nights when classroom filler was needed. It is simplistic in nature, easy to draw up on the white board, and also intuitive in nature. In retrospect, one may ask, why didn't I pursue the line of inquiry to expose the fraudulent claims of the psychologist? And I would have to admit, I wasn't too keen on verifying the accusations against Maslow because not only did I enjoy reciting the theory, but intuitively it made good sense and therefore should work that way.

Ignoring the controversy of the theory's validity and unbeknownst to Maslow at the time, a cottage industry was born, revolving around the word "motivation." Overnight, theories of motivation sprang to life. Rats became a desired commodity, speaker bureaus were a buzz, and workshop venues were at a premium. A new breed of consultant reared its ugly head that continues to this day, the motivational speaker.

In addition to the widespread use of the term motivation, another twenty-first century term that has gained wide acceptance in the lexicon of the businessman's vocabulary is the term "engagement."

According to *Talent Management* magazine (August 2014), many cite the arrival of the term "engagement," and insertion into the management lexicon with a 1999 *Institute for Employment Studies* article, which examined the link between frontline worker happiness and customer satisfaction in the service industry.

Employee Engagement is defined as "the emotional commitment to the organization and its goals." In the past, an engaged employee would be referred to as one willing to go that extra mile for the team. Researchers in the field frequently note that the use of "we" opposed to "me" is one of the speech patterns of the truly engaged employee. Similar to motivation, engagement has such a positive and desirable overtone and it is hard to imagine one not supportive of its suggested outcomes. In clarifying the definition, the engaged employee is further recognized for one's behaviors in discretionary situations. The difficulty of defining what is and is not a discretionary effort is more of a challenge. If people stoop to pick up trash that has been carelessly discarded in the parking lot, are they doing so out of love and commitment to the company, or are they merely environmentally self-conscious?

The attraction to engagement is the same as the attraction to motivation. What's not to like? They both reek of optimism and future positive outcomes. Both have a deterministic quality that is hard not to support and comfortably project anticipated outcomes supported by research in their respective fields.

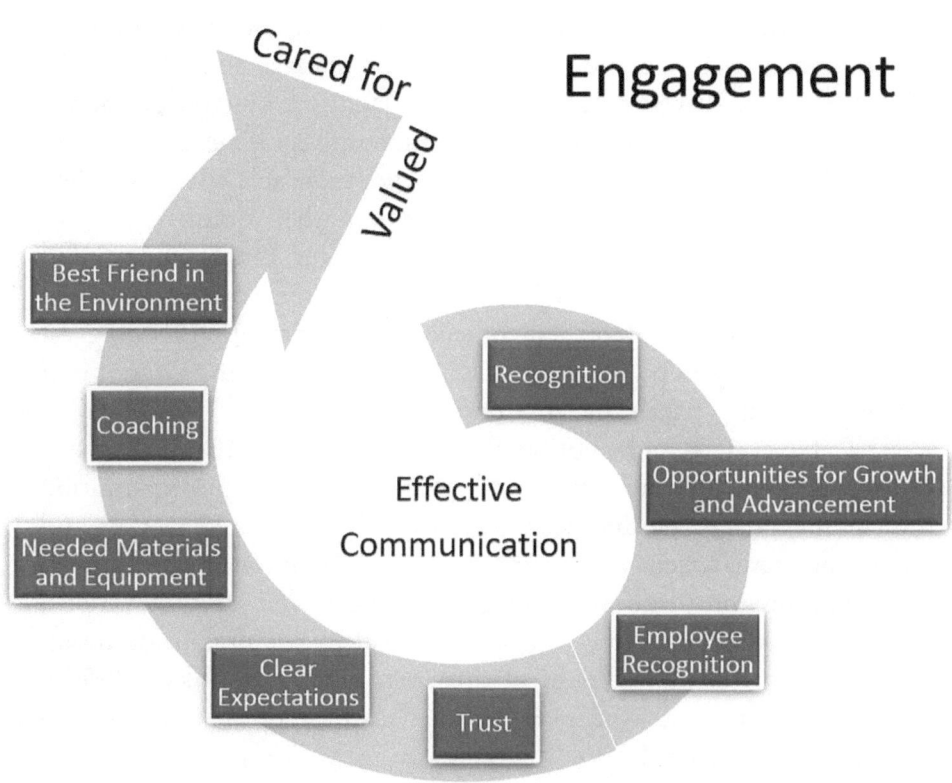

Drivers to Engagement

The characteristics or environmental traits that contribute or influence an environment supporting an atmosphere conducive to engagement are referred to as drivers. These drivers will vary in degree of emphasis and frequency of delivery but are recognized to be the distinguishing quality or characteristics of engagement.

The major drivers of engagement are effective communication, continuous employee recognition, opportunities for employee growth and advancement, and an overall atmosphere of trust amongst employees as well as between employees and management.

Secondary drivers to engagement are clearly defined expectations of the employee, availability of materials and equipment needed to meet the established expectations, and knowledgeable coaching when needed. Engaged employees must sense that their opinions are not only heard but valued by the administrative team. Employees respond favorably when they feel cared about and when their progress is noted by their supervisor or management team. Current research also suggest engaged employees perform better when they have a significant or best friend working in the same environment.

To be engaged and emotionally committed to an organization and its goals is to anticipate a variety of positive results for the organization including greater productivity, higher profits, increased worker and customer satisfaction, customer loyalty and retention, lower rates of absenteeism and turnover, fewer quality defects and safety violations, and a considerable degree of customer loyalty. The organization will also benefit from lower rates of turnover, product shrinkage (theft), quality defects, and work place accidents. Once again, what's not to like? Everybody wins!

Benefits of Engagement

Benefits:
- Greater Productivity
- Higher Profits
- Customer Satisfaction
- Customer Loyalty
- Lower Absenteeism
- Fewer Quality Defects
- Higher Retention and Worker Satisfaction
- Increased shareholder value

Engagement
"The emotional commitment to the organization and its goals"

Research supporting the above claims is readily available and abundant. Kevin Kruse's book, *Employee Engagement 2.0 (2012)*, is an excellent resource containing 28 research findings demonstrating a correlation between employee engagement and the desired outcomes mentioned above. For backup, I always carry his earlier work co-authored with Rudy Karsan, *How To Increase Performance and Profits Through Full Engagement (2011)*. This book is also an excellent resource based on research from Kenexa, a company that conducts employee engagement and opinion surveys for more than 10 million workers in over 150 countries each year. I figured that was an adequate sampling; however, if truth be known, I have rarely been questioned regarding the legitimacy of the claims made by experts in the field of engagement. I suspect the reason for that is the concept is so appealing intuitively. What manager or owner would state that it wasn't of interest or importance to them to increase productivity, profits, etc.?

As a consultant in the field of employee engagement, I have come to some conclusions relating to the overall process of evaluating current rates of engagement as well as introducing steps to improve future levels of engagement. The primary method for determining current rates of engagement is the administration of a survey, electronic or paper/pencil, and conducted by a member of the human resources department.

I would strongly advise against utilizing in-house personnel or utilizing an electronic survey instrument for a couple of reasons. It has been my experience that the most prevalent factor leading to disengagement is a breakdown of communication within the organization. Surrounding this breakdown in communication is frequently an atmosphere of distrust. Now which came first, the breakdown in communication or the distrust, can become a chicken and egg discussion, but is somewhat irrelevant. At this point, they feed off one another, and any attempt to gather pertinent data from individuals or technology that may be traceable within the organization is met with a great deal of skepticism at best. Nevertheless, any results or future efforts to enhance engagement will be met with resistance given the questionable origin and reliability of the data. Save yourself the trouble; go outside the organization for data collection.

Most of the literature relating to engagement will suggest an organization is better off not introducing initial engagement surveys or efforts relating to engagement if there is no intent to follow up on the findings that result. I disagree with this. I have found there to be tremendous value in hiring outside expertise in the field to come in to an organization and simultaneously conduct an employee interview while administering the survey instrument. The interview may be very broad in nature, inquiring about what brought an employee to the organization, how they have progressed, what challenges they have encountered and what suggestions and/or recommendations they may have to make the work environment more pleasant and productive.

The opportunity to merely express their concerns and be heard is of tremendous value to the employee. And to keep it in perspective, the truth of the matter is employee expectations are rather modest with respect to any outcomes or expectations that may materialize as a result of their engagement interview. However, that doesn't negate the benefits to be derived from the experience. For the most part, employees have worked for years victims of policies dictated from above. To be heard by an independent party is perceived to be a giant step forward for most employees.

I recently interviewed more than 1,500 employees from a very successful company in a somewhat isolated area representing a population of 8,600 residents. I discovered what I consider to be another significant driver of engagement that others involved in engagement theory have not introduced, and that is the impact of geographic isolation as it relates to engagement.

Assume that an organization is located in a very remote and isolated area and has a very competitive salary and a Cadillac of a benefits package. The conversation relating to alternative employment opportunities, if desired, takes on a completely different tone. If one desires to change employment for any particular reason, it becomes a much greater issue than merely adjusting one's commute to a different location. If one wants to match both salary and benefits, it means physical relocating and all that accompanies that decision.

Geographical isolation appears to encourage engagement or the emotional commitment to the organization because the loss of employment would be so devastating to the lifestyle established. Ironically, this isolation may even be detrimental to some of the other key drivers of engagement like communication and trust. One may be hesitant to confide in a fellow worker or express discontentment of any manner, in fear of personality conflicts in the future, or reprisal, possibly in the form of dismissal. In short, when there is little, if any, comparable competition in the area, employees may experience a great deal of fear or mistrust, nevertheless rating the organization relatively high on factors relating to engagement (work satisfaction, alternative job searching, recommending the current employer).

For most employees, an engagement event will be the first and last time someone has sincerely asked for their input regarding the workplace. And this observation includes annual reviews conducted by supervisors, etc., bearing in mind the earlier observation that most bureaucracies exist in an atmosphere girdled in mistrust and poor communication, not to mention the in-house personnel conducting the interview may easily be the major bone of contention.

For those employees who are intimidated by the one-on-one interview seeking their input for suggestions and new ideas, I would recommend having a copy of Sam Parker's book, *212 the Extra Degree*, on hand. This compact little handbook illustrates the reality that heating water to 211 degrees produces very hot water, but adding just one more degree of heat takes it to 212 degrees and it boils, producing the steam energy sufficient to power a locomotive. What appears to be a small, tiny increment of change may trigger major changes having lasting impact on an organization.

For example, I recently witnessed the impact that introducing a shuttle for employees to their vehicles had on an organization located in northern Minnesota, granted that walk to the car following the night shift may hover in the sub-zero range as the wind whips across the plains in northern Minnesota. It's gestures like this that contribute to employees feeling "safe," the desirable state employees seek that James Hunter refers to in his book, *The Servant*. This "I've got your back" feeling from the management team is what employees long for and is certainly a characteristic of an engaged work environment. Employees feel valued in such an atmosphere.

With regard to the observation that one would be better off doing nothing than asking for input with no follow through, most employees have such low expectations that anything will ever result from their input, it is very hard to disappoint them by a limited response. Unfortunately, the bar is set very low in most instances, and employees are grateful just for the opportunity to express their concerns.

I frequently advise companies that are aware of high levels of disengagement (usually evident by high turnover) but may not have the funds or are unwilling to conduct the initial survey to first determine the specific areas where drivers are deficient to invest in training their supervisors. The relationship between the employee and their immediate supervisor is the primary key to high levels of engagement. If this relationship is not solid, there will continue to be a heavy, if not terminal effect on the organization. This applies to all levels of supervision within the organization.

The immediate question from the administration is in what areas should the training for the supervisors be directed? I pause to reflect on how most supervisors obtained their positions and sadly reflect on the dark side of that mobility. Most supervisors obtain their current positions by excelling in the task consistent with their previous position. Success and competence in performance yields promotion, frequently to supervisor. Unfortunately, the down side of this popular mobility phenomenon was exposed nearly fifty years ago by a Canadian academic, Laurence J. Peter in his best seller, *The Peter Principle (1969)*.

The Peter Principle states that managers rise to their level of incompetence. They are continuously promoted until they fail to do well in their current job. The final promotion is from a level of competence to a level of incompetence. In short, people are promoted to a level of incompetence, and this is when the promotions cease. This promotion is unfortunate for those whom the newly promoted will now supervise.

The second most popular avenue to a supervisory role or upper management position is to be an individual who interviews well. Again, this ability to interview well is no certainty that one will perform well, just recognition that they interview well. In any event, when the interview is the primary or sole criteria for promotion, there shouldn't be a great deal of surprise from the administration when there is a breakdown in communication between employee and supervisor resulting in disengagement or lack of emotional commitment to the organization. Frequently, the reward for doing a mechanical or technical job well is to be promoted to a position that requires an entirely new set of skills, including interpersonal skills, with minimal or limited training. This lack of skills and preparation in interpersonal relations frequently results in a defensive demeanor from the newly appointed supervisor who is fearful of being exposed.

In response to the training question, what would you suggest we do to bring our supervisors up to speed? At the risk of dating myself, I would quickly suggest Dale Carnegie's, *How to Win Friends and Influence People* book and course. Too often I see organizations clamoring for the latest management theory or technique in order to bring the skills of their management team up to date. What's needed has stood the test of time, given the predictability of people, and their desire to feel important and appreciated. These are basic, basic skills, but unfortunately never taught and frequently overlooked. Check out Carnegie's table of contents:

Give honest, sincere appreciation;
Arouse in the other person an eager want;
The only way to get the best of an argument is to avoid it;
Show respect for the other person's opinions. Never say, "You're Wrong."
Ask questions instead of giving direct orders;
Let the other person save face.

This is just a sampling of the interpersonal skills to which most supervisors have had limited exposure. All efforts directed toward the refinement of these interpersonal skills are a tremendous step toward closing the communication gap that exists.

Eventually, as directors of HR and concerned parties extend efforts to identify or recognize what it is within their organizations that is causing low morale, high turnover, and a plethora of other undesirable outcomes, they will conclude the culprit to be "poor communication." In an effort to save countless hours of internal examination, I would like to offer a quick fix based on decades of experience in the field.

Enemy number one to ineffective communication will most likely be incomplete information.

Perhaps I should be more explicit. Information is incomplete when it does not specifically relate to the needs, wants, and desires of the employee. Employees simply want to know, how can you and/or your solution help me? Period! They are not concerned about the resources you have access to, your success within the industry, or your market share. When new policies, rules, and regulations are introduced, employees would like a courtesy reminder of what is currently being done, know **why** a change has been initiated, **how** it will be implemented, and lastly, **how it will affect them personally.** They simply want to know how your solution will make it a better world for them. Anything else is propaganda.

The diagram below illustrates how new policies are typically introduced, followed by an illustration of the way employees prefer to receive new information. If they choose to avoid the more detailed explanation, they can be assured of an avalanche of water-cooler discussion attempting to decipher who, how, and why the change was introduced. These discussion points are inevitable, and until they are resolved in the mind of the employee, there will be degrees of resistance and sabotage regarding the change.

Policy Change Example

Effective Communication

What if there was an established procedure that every new policy, rule, and regulation introduced contained these four elements of explanation: present procedure, need for change, how it will work and lastly how it would affect the employee? This is the type of communication that employees seek. This is how employees begin to feel valued, and this type of communication instills commitment, support, loyalty, and involvement that contributes to the overall atmosphere of trust, a fundamental cornerstone to engagement. This closes the communication gap between supervisor and employee drastically.

I'm sure some would argue that employees are informed on a "need to know bases," and this approach will slow down the communication process. I think initially this is true; however, in the end, the long range benefits outweigh the immediacy of implementation. Think of it in terms of teaching a child. "Just do it!" may influence immediate action, but it will be temporary, challenged and a constant source of debate beginning with the inevitable question of Why? Why? Why?

In addition to incomplete information contributing to the communication gap, enemy number two would be not communicating within the desired learning channel of the employee. According to research conducted by Neuro Linguistic Programing (NLP) practitioner, it is vital to recognize that individuals have a preferred learning channel when receiving new information. Some desire information in a verbal form, others prefer visual stimulation, and others are more kinesthetic in nature. It is not up to the source or originator of the information to determine which channel is the preferred channel but to assure that all three channels are addressed or activated. No doubt my verbal explanation of Maslow's Hierarchy of Needs was acceptable to the auditory learners, and I'm sure the visual learners appreciated the diagram. To reach the kinesthetic learners who need to be more actively involved in the learning process, I would need to get them more physically active, perhaps asking them to either place a dot on the pyramid to indicate their present stage of development or write specific actions that would indicate their involvement at each level of development. The physical action of writing engages the kinesthetic mind.

In order to make communication relevant to the receivers, they must be able to clearly identify why the suggested change is taking place, how it will occur, how it affects them, and ideally presented in a manner conducive to how they learn best, whether it be visual, auditory, or kinesthetic.

The ability to communicate to a specific learning channel other than one preferred by the individual sending the message can be more challenging than first anticipated. As a visual learner myself, I make it a practice to have clients draw as we begin our interview. I resort to some standby expressions in order to make this happen. I may ask an engineer (frequently kinesthetic) to "Illustrate to me where you fit into the organization or illustrate where you see the conflict," or "Show me where the bottleneck exists." I will always have some props near in order to convert a visual explanation to a kinesthetic explanation. I never apologize for the request, and if I see any hesitation, I merely request, "I'm a visual learner and in order to better assist you, I need an illustration."

As authority figures continue to choose to be comfortable opposed to effective in their communication, it is inevitable that they will continue to be dysfunctional. This phenomenon, blatantly observed in bureaucracies, introduces enemy number three, the development silos of information. In silos, information becomes the currency and therefore only shared with those individuals or departments that have similar views and goals. Many consider this non-transparent silo environment as not so much a matter of personalities each seeking to be heard but simply a lack of shared direction. The only way to break through these silos, short of cleaning house, is to pursue common goals that require team participation. In most bureaucracies where there is frequently an absence of trust as well as an avoidance of accountability, a positive outcome is difficult at best but not impossible. In the absence of commitment, the communication gap will only become wider.

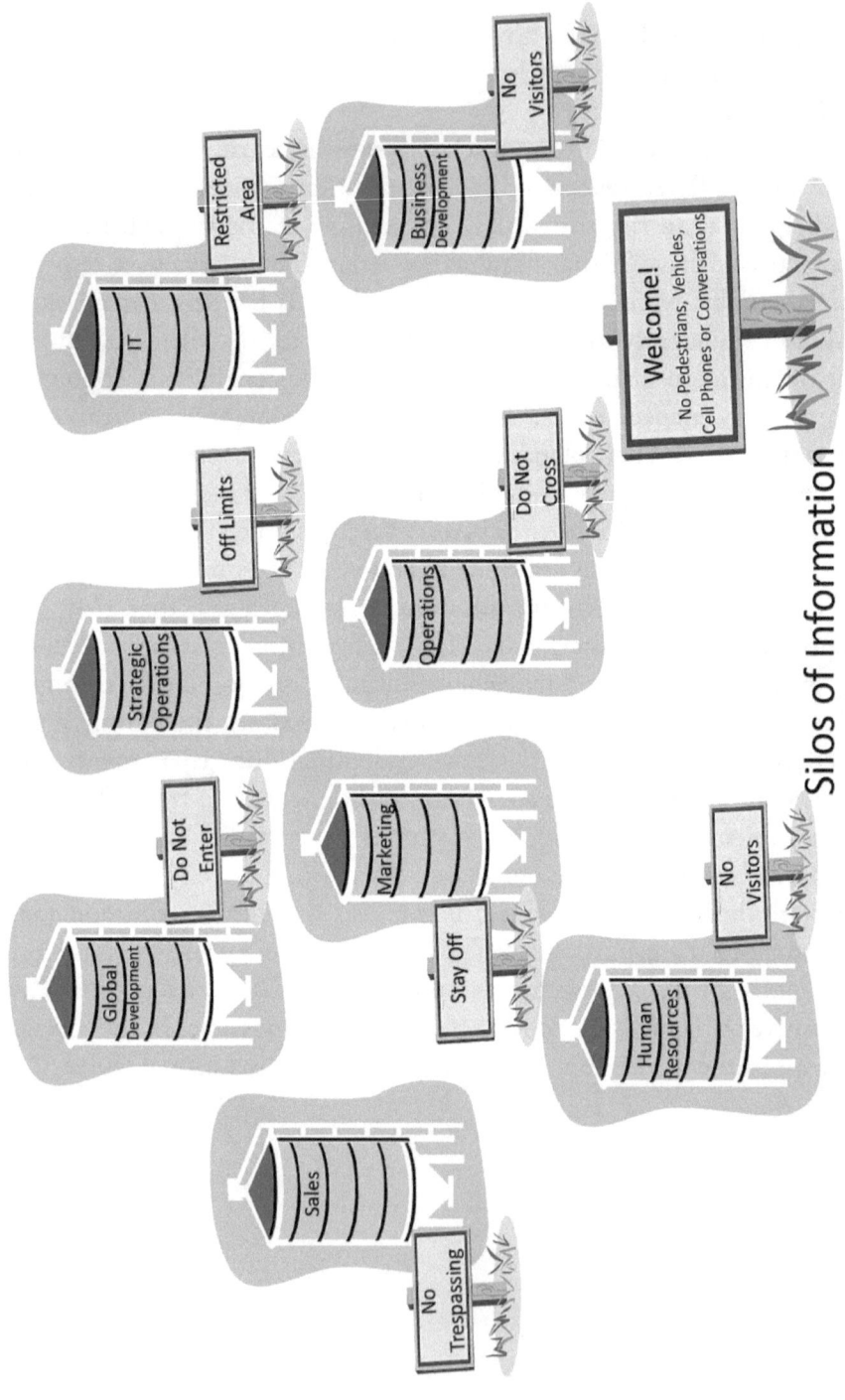

Silos of Information

Lencioni, has done an admirable job outlining the end result of this sort of turf/information protectiveness in his book, *The 5 Dysfunction of a Team.* He identifies the glaring evidence when a team is dysfunctional by identifying the five major dysfunctions of a team: lack of commitment, fear of conflict, avoidance of accountability, inattention to results, and lack of trust. It has been my professional experience and opinion that it becomes relatively easy to predict which escape route will be exercised by any given authority figure in order to maintain an appearance of cooperation and avoid any hint of not being a team player. Modifying Lencioni's options, meetings take on the atmosphere of attempting to guess which avenue or exit will be taken (see illustration below).

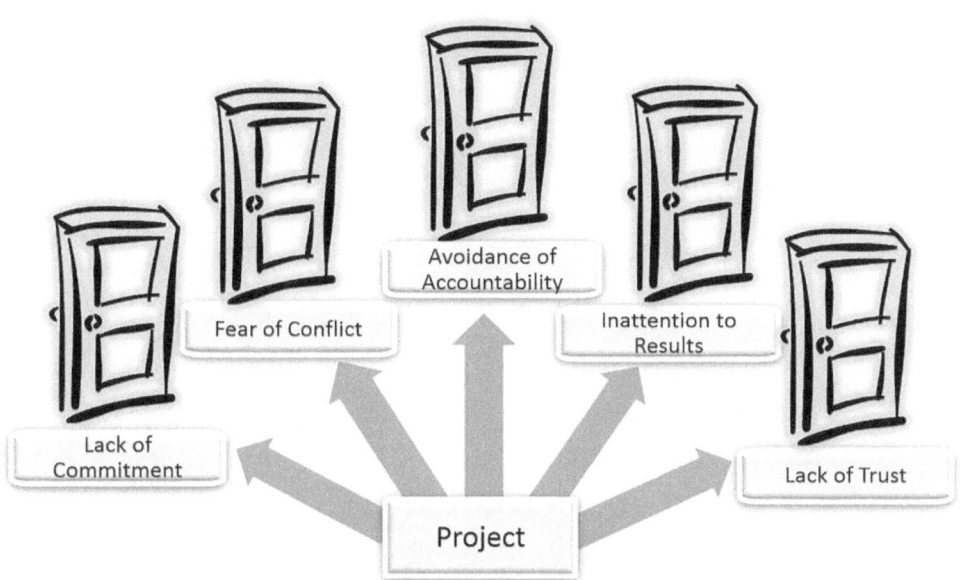

Pick your Escape Route

Lencioni's Dysfunctions of a Team

Individual mannerisms, limited contributions, and excuses serve to reveal an individual's favorite escape route rather easily. Lencioni identifies the five doors above as repercussions of a dysfunctional team that become barriers that turn colleagues into competitors. I would suggest that they are also well worn escape routes that stifle the exchange of information and make the communication gap wider still.

The earlier in the process one detects the desired exit route of a team member, the less disappointing it will be as projects lag, delays are prevalent, and results are postponed for no apparent reason. Let us return to the classroom.

SECTION 2

PERCEIVED VALUE

"Dr. Haviland, would you consider an executive's ability to establish a high level of engagement the key to making them worth almost $500.00 an hour?" The class, Emerging Patterns of Leadership, was a graduate class in the public administration program.

"What makes you ask, and why did you pick that hourly rate?" I inquired.

"Well, the most recent edition of Forbes Magazine has released the salaries and compensation of the leading CEO's, and a lot of these guys are making more than $1,000,000 a year."

"Yes, that's probably true, but where does the $500.00 an hour come into play?"

"That was my calculation. I calculated a forty hour work week for fifty-two weeks a year and came up with two thousand and eighty hours of work in a year. I divided the million a year salary by the two thousand and eighty hours worked and came up with over $400.00 an hour, $480.76, to be precise."

"That sounds accurate," I responded, still trying to figure out where this was going and conscious of the fact this discussion had little to do with my lesson plan. Nevertheless, the other members of the class seemed to enjoy the exchange. *"Do you think most CEOs only work a forty hour week?"* I challenged.

"No, I think most would claim they work a lot more, but this doesn't really reflect holidays, a minimum of four weeks for vacation and a boatload of other bennies we all know they get. Think of it, these guys make over one hundred and fifteen dollars when they take a fifteen minute coffee break. It just doesn't seem fair."

This was a moment frozen in time for me. Quite frankly, I don't recall exactly how the exchange between the two of us ended some twenty-five years ago. However, I suspect I said something relating to the dynamics of compensation and leadership in an attempt to lead us back to the syllabus and the lecture I had planned for the evening.

The exchange that evening remains a bench mark, not only due to the emotional trauma I experienced my first night teaching graduate school, but more importantly a deep seated and to some extent unconscious concern that I had harbored for some twenty-five years and would continue to research for the next twenty-five years. How could one person be so much more valuable to an organization than another? And more pointedly, how could I become that person? The mystery lay before me. My quest became to solve the mystery of what constitutes individual financial value or worth to an organization and to discern how this dynamic or trait is transferred to personal relationships. If in fact this trait is transferable to personal relationships, it becomes priceless. This book reflects the journey experienced in solving the mystery. Enjoy the journey. Enjoy the future.

Unbeknownst to my father, he was a significant influence on me and my quest to uncover the dynamics of leadership. From his earlier years as a boyhood farmer in Iowa, he became a door-to-door salesman of pots and pans. I envisage him as an outgoing, gregarious sociable salesman of the Elmer Gantry or Music Man's Professor Howard Hill mold. My father attended Morningside College in Iowa and was the captain of the football team, president of his class, a member of the debate team, and as my mother would attest, *"A striking handsome clothes hound, with the whitest shirts I've ever seen."*

My father went to Creighton Medical School and as the story goes, due to the Depression era times, he was not financially able to continue with his education. As our family began, he became the breadwinner. My earliest memories of him were as a postman and a night bartender, with a sideline of selling pots and pans. I include this historical footnote as a reflection on a man who was extremely competent and proud. Yet due to financial hardships and a growing family, he had to sacrifice his dreams and leave them behind. Not once did I ever hear him resort to the "pity party" of how unfair the world had been to him. When we traveled down memory lane and he reflected on his life, he would admit; *"The biggest mistake I ever made was being too proud to ask others for help when I needed it. I can only imagine how our lives would have been different."*

My father did not lose his ability to enjoy the company of others. I was envious of the way he could attract others to him. One particular insight became instrumental in my quest to discover the mysterious traits of leadership. In my youth, along with my two brothers, we delivered the morning *Detroit Free Press* to the homes and businesses in our town of Drayton Plains, Michigan approximately thirty miles north of Detroit. I would collect payment on Friday evenings when most people were home; however, there was also a hidden agenda for collecting late on Fridays. I delivered to one favorite lounge that was particularly warm and friendly to me, primarily because my father was the bartender.

I would enter in about eight in the evening, saunter up to the bar and request payment for the *Detroit Free Press*. My father would lean over the bar and tell me to take a seat at the little table at the far end of the bar and he would get to me as soon as possible. "In the meantime, would I like a coke as I waited?" This charade would play out week after week. And I loved every minute of it, especially near Christmas when the bar lights would be twinkling, frequently highlighting the sounds from a little combo playing up front, and the hum of conversation would blend with the constant laughter and tinkle of ice cubes against glass. Dad was well known in these parts because he delivered mail and sold pots and pans door-to-door in addition to bartending.

The table would frequently fill with friends as I enjoyed the music, the laughter, and the commotion. The conversation would jump from sports to politics to local events and inevitably, usually about the time we were about to leave, out of the blue one of the customers would yell out, "Say Paul, round me up a set of those three saucepans, will ya?" The pans that Dad peddled during the day were conveniently on display at the back of the bar. "It'll be great as a surprise."

"*I'll drop them off Tuesday, and say hi to Carol,*" Dad would respond. Having experienced this transaction on several occasions, I was forced to make a confession to my dad.

"*Dad, I don't get it. I never hear you trying to sell anybody anything. I never hear you talking about pots and pans. Yet several times when we walk out, somebody puts in an order for pots and pans.*" He let out a big laugh.

"Son, rarely is it about the product. They can get the same set of pans right down the street or one that's lighter weight and cheaper at the hardware."

"So why do they buy from you?" I asked.

"It's all about relationships son. It's all about relationships," he grinned. "I'll explain it when we get home."

That evening we settled down for hot chocolate at the kitchen table, and he gave me his threadbare copy of Dale Carnegie's *How to Win Friends and Influence People*.

"Son, when you read this, you'll understand what I meant when I said it's not about the product. Next to the Bible, this is the most important book you'll ever read in your life. Far more important than anything I ever read in college."

I have been hooked since that day and remain a lifetime fan of Carnegie. Ironically, Carnegie supplied a discussion point of the graduate class as other members of the class began to contribute.

"*Do you think a CEO is that far superior to the rest of us?*" A young woman asked. This prompted another student to inquire.

"*Are they that smart or technologically savvy?*"

It was now more than a quarter of a century since I had read Carnegie for the first time, and yet this was an opportune moment for me to quote one of the studies from the Carnegie Institute of Technology.

According to Carnegie, "*Investigations revealed that even in such technical lines as engineering, about 15 percent of one's financial success is due to one's technical knowledge and about 85 percent is due to skill in human engineering—to personality and the ability to lead people."*

"*That's only one study,*" a skeptical voice from the back of the room shouted.

"*No, as I recall, Zig Ziglar quotes the Carnegie study and references three other reputable institutions that replicated the Carnegie study, resulting in the same statistical outcomes.*" I welcomed this opportunity to sound professorial and to capture a fraction of my investment in higher education which focused exclusively on theories of leadership.

"*Dr. Haviland, do you think it's the CEO's personality or the CEO's ability to lead that makes them so valuable?*"

"*Would it sound like a cop-out if I said I think it's a combination of the two? I believe that some individuals possess a personality trait that enables them to lead more effectively than others. Does that work for you?*"

"*I don't know. Is it a trait that can be identified with a price tag put on it?*" He asked.

"*I'm not sure the specific trait has been identified, but some feel that the end result, the ability to lead, carries a price tag. John D. Rockefeller said, 'The ability to deal with people is as purchasable a commodity as sugar or coffee. And I will pay more for that ability, than for any other under the sun.' Pretty strong endorsement, I would say.*" And this endorsement is certainly consistent with the earlier discussions relating to engagement, Carnegie, and my father.

SECTION 3

THE IVORY TOWER

I was amazed. At this point we hadn't touched on any topic that I had so laboriously outlined for the evening. Nor had I even passed out the course syllabus. My plan was to hand out the syllabus and then very diligently proceed to outline in great detail the requirements of the class pertaining to attendance, grading, etc. I planned to answer any questions they may have had, anticipating there would be none, and then dismiss early to offer them an opportunity for the purchase of texts at the bookstore. Thus, my first evening as a "college prof" would be complete.

Personally, I always resented that first night script endorsed by the vast majority of college professors, but like most students, I accepted it. It always seemed frustrating to interrupt my evening activities (not that they were so productive) to travel to campus and be dismissed ten minutes later. After the first freshman semester, most students assumed that would be the routine and wouldn't bother to bring pencil or paper to the first class. Students learn that they are expected to be excited when early dismissal is announced, as if in elementary school a "snow-day" had been proclaimed. Insult was added to injury when a graduate student was assigned the "opening night task" and the lead professor reserved grand entrance rights for the second scheduled class session. I've always believed that in the event a substitute graduate assistant or GA served as a stand-in for the assigned professor, I should receive a rebate. This rebate would also apply if a class were cancelled, especially if the class was cancelled so the "professor could attend a conference." I'm not sure how that was ever a benefit to me.

Another one of my favorite rituals was an instructor who required seven textbooks for the course in an effort to convey the rigorous discipline needed to master the subject material. This instructor proceeded to casually reference two of the textbooks on three isolated occasions during the semester. Ultimately, the students would perform the ritual of returning the unopened books for a discounted refund. By the sophomore year, most students learned that writing their name in the front of the book would only reduce the amount of refund received; therefore, they avoided the ritual. The insult was only magnified when one of the required texts was authored by the instructor and written seventeen years ago when he or she was seeking tenure.

I don't consider myself to be a cynic of higher education; however, to say I am highly skeptical would be an understatement. I have taught at every level of education from high school to graduate school and served as a dean, vice provost, provost, and president of a college. I have witnessed most of the rituals and scams that are in play. The textbook scam mentioned is renewed annually and justified due to the reality that most students receive grants-in-aid; therefore, it "isn't really money out of their pockets." The reality of student loans resulting in massive student debt in the future is reserved for later discussion. The cost of textbooks pales in comparison to the cost of housing and tuition.

Escalating tuition cost goes unchecked because it usually requires state or system-wide approval, i.e., legislative approval. Legislators' grant approval because they don't want to defend an anti-education platform in their next campaign. Legislators are always readily aware of the quasi-united front that faculty represent. This remains a threat to legislators because faculty represent high voter turnout, may unite if threatened, and are very articulate in expressing their discontent should it be necessary. Isn't it just easier to go along with the flow? For independent institutions that don't require legislative approval for tuition hikes, it's easier to let the state institutions do the heavy lifting first and then adjust tuition upward in their shadow. It continues to be a vicious cycle with no end in sight.

Just a few more words on higher education prior to returning to the opening night class discussion. As an adjunct instructor, as well as the early years as a faculty member, it has been my observation that one does not immediately feel totally accepted by the fraternity of fellow faculty members. And this is to be expected. As an adjunct with limited resources, one is appreciative of the opportunity to share a secretary or possibly office space in order to post office hours (required but seldom honored). The primary concern of many instructors is to be within ten minutes of the scheduled class time and hopefully find a parking space. The other concern is to exit as fast as possible in order to return to their day job and trust that their absence has not been noticed.

For a newly appointed faculty member, the focus is on doing whatever is requested in order to "fit in" and to progress toward tenure. Although cordial, one's colleagues do not view the new faculty member as an equal for a variety of reasons. They are not sure of that person's commitment to the institution. This may be merely a steppingstone for one seeking appointment at a more prestigious school. Also, the newly appointed faculty members have not proven themselves by contributing publications to a "refereed journal." For the layperson, a "refereed journal" or publication reflects the content of a given discipline, and articles are reviewed and selected for publication by a committee of experts within the field. Many academics view this as the critical component contributing to tenure.

Initially as an adjunct gaining experience, and subsequently with my first full time faculty member appointment at another institution, I accepted this indifference and attributed it to the rookie experience. I was amused by the fact that three campus cars would be reserved for three faculty members all attending the same conference. The fact that many of the faculty members preferred to bring a sandwich from home and eat in the confines of their office with the door shut, opposed to dining in the faculty dining room, reflects this desire to withdraw.

As I entered the administrative ranks which required more intricate interaction among the faculty, I became aware of the fact that many of the faculty members didn't particularly care for one another. To suggest any social communication or supporting comment toward "The Administration" is flirting with the label of "traitor" to the faculty union. As I continued my progression through three community colleges and three universities, I realized this animosity between faculty and administration was not the exception but the rule.

This friction became more apparent as I began the scheduling of courses for the institution. Faculty were most cooperative and flexible with the scheduling of courses, provided their classes would meet between the hours of ten and two o'clock in the afternoon, on Monday, Wednesday, and Friday, if necessary. An evening class was acceptable, only if required in the contract. They were totally supportive of evening, weekend, and extension classes, providing they were not the ones assigned to teach the class. The faculty bristled at the suggestion that adjunct faculty members be hired to fill any available teaching slots. Adjunct faculty members were frequently seen as a threat to tenured faculty, primarily because they enjoyed students and the opportunity to teach.

Eventually it became very apparent that not only did the faculty not like each other or the administration, but they didn't care much for the students either, and by default, the institution as a whole. This observation was very bothersome to me early in my career prior to my exposure to two significant contributions from others who had walked in my shoes. The first was an article entitled, "A Discourse on Professorial Melancholia," written by David F. Machell and published in Community Review, by the City University of New York.

Machell does an excellent job of explaining how and why there is such a disconnect between faculty members and those to whom they are indebted. He succinctly outlines the journey to which most faculty members fall victim. Most faculty members aspire to join the profession because they have a deep-seated love for their discipline. Due to their junior status, new faculty are frequently assigned to teach the intro-level classes within the discipline, while the more intriguing topics are reserved for senior-level or graduate-level faculty. Unfortunately, the intro-level classes are frequently required classes; therefore, the bulk of attendees are students who have a marginal interest in the subject at best. The primary concern of the student is usually about test content only.

Secondly, the disappointment relating to the limited attention span of the freshman students is intensified by the lack of support from fellow faculty members. This along with extended commitments including committee participation and the need to publish or perish in order to influence tenure opportunities combine to form the perfect storm.

Let's return to the classroom.

SECTION 4

LEADERSHIP: SUCCESS/ WEALTH/FAME

"*Of all the characteristics required of a leader, which one do you consider to be the most important?*"

"*That's a thought provoking question. Let's expand it to the class. I'd like to hear what you think.*" I was pleased to note the entire class was fully engaged at this point.

"*Charisma, Self-confidence, 'Visionary,*" came the responses.

"*Slow down; let me list them on the board,*" I pleaded and began the list:

49

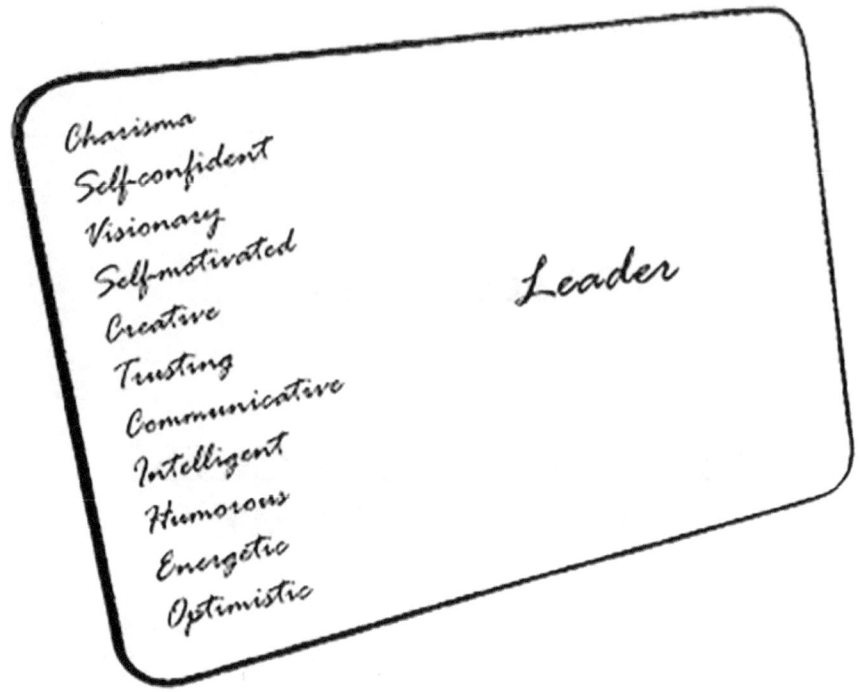

"Does that do it?" I questioned.

"It's a good start," was the response.

"Is it possible to find all of these traits in one person?" I inquired.

"Possibly, but rarely. If you did, that person would be a saint," was the response.

"Perhaps that's the point that Rockefeller was trying to make. This combination of traits and the ability to lead is so rare it is virtually priceless. What would it mean to an organization to have someone at the helm with these characteristics? I challenged.

"At least $480.00 an hour!" was the immediate answer.

"So here's your challenge. Utilizing your brain power along with that of two others sitting near you, assume you want this 'ideal CEO' but can't afford the million-a-year price tag. I want you to identify which two traits you would be willing to sacrifice in order to stay within budget and which one you consider to be absolutely essential. Select a spokesperson and we will hear your group's justification in fifteen minutes."

The room began to buzz with conversation as students began introducing themselves to their newly appointed teammates and began to jockey for reasons why they couldn't or shouldn't be the spokesperson for the group. In the hallway, I caught the eye of another rookie faculty member as he was exiting for the evening. He had this incredulous expression as he viewed the listing on the board and noticed the commotion of the students in the room.

I felt like I had broken some sort of sacred pedagogical pact by stepping out of the brotherhood and actually teaching the first night of class. I anticipated I would hear from the Dean that week and be reprimanded by the brotherhood. I didn't care, and I was feeling pretty good about what was taking place. The activity was no reflection of what I had planned for the first night, nor was there anything on the syllabus indicating any level of participation required, but I was feeling worthy to teach this special topics course, *Emerging Patterns of Leadership!*

"Who would like to begin?" I invited. Silence. "All right, for five dollars, who knows the capital of Delaware?" I advanced the five dollars from my pocket and a hand immediately shot up and simultaneously called out, *"Dover."*

"Would anyone like to challenge that?" I petitioned. "Hearing no objections, may I ask your name?"

"Glenn Wright"

"Well, thank you, Mr. Wright. *That answer provides you with two opportunities. First, the five dollars is yours, and secondly, you have the opportunity to represent your group and share your choice of the traits you would be willing to sacrifice in a CEO and also that one trait you deem absolutely essential."*

"May I be creative in my response and suggest I only receive four dollars and another group go first?" he responded. The class laughed and cheered his response as he made his way to the front of the room.

"No deal, but good try." I offered. *"How did you know Dover?"* I asked.

"My grandmother lives there and we made the journey every summer since I was knee high to a grasshopper," he offered.

"Sounds reasonable. Please, share with us what your group came up with, Mr. Wright."

"After much deliberation and in order to have some response, we decided self-confidence and self-motivation were the two traits we were willing to sacrifice in the CEO." The murmurs of disagreement were audible.

"Hang on. You'll get your chance," I coached. "How did you and your group come to this conclusion, Mr. Wright?" I needled.

"We considered these two traits possible by-products or end products that may not be essential up front, but given time and some opportunities for success, they were traits that would be developed and acquired?" he urged.

"So, would that be a question or a statement, Mr. Wright?" I quizzed.

"Let's see. I already have the five dollars, don't I?" Laughter and I nodded. "*That being the case, I would like to offer that up as a statement of fact,*" Wright inserted.

"Would anyone like to refute that?" I hinted.

"What makes you think there would be any success without those traits?" a voice from the back.

"And your name is?" I asked.

"Brittany Reynolds," she responded.

"Thank you, Miss Reynolds. Mr. Wright, it's all yours."

"Yea, well, we had a problem with that also."

"Jeff, another member of our group also had some concerns."

"Please identify yourself, Jeff." He raised his hand and we applauded.

"Well, perhaps Jeff can explain it better." It was obvious Jeff was caught off guard, as he made his way to the front. "Or as they say, it's all yours, Jeff."

"Thanks, Glenn. I'll remember this."

"Well, we looked at success from a different perspective and concluded; most people would consider winning the lottery or driving to work and arriving on time as successful ventures. Both activities can be completed successfully and don't require any measurable degree of self-confidence or self-motivation. However, accomplishing either or both, over a given amount of time, would no doubt be considered a success, and both traits would grow over time but not be necessary initially.

Glenn jumped back in. *"Or think of a pro athlete or accomplished musician. They may have a raw talent, but lack confidence or motivation; however, after they compete on several occasions, both traits may become clearly obvious."* This response generated a rowdy applause for the two. With ample grins of satisfaction, they shook hands and began their exit to their seats.

"Excellent. And may I pause for a teaching moment?" I urged at the same time I took center stage. *"Let me ask this. Did either Glenn's or Jeff's self-confidence grow as a result of that exchange?"* Most nodded approvingly. *"So we would consider this a successful experience for them?"* More agreement from the class

"Now consider this. Was there any evidence of self-motivation on their part prior to be being selected, aside from Glenn's desire for the five dollars?" Most indicated no. *"Therefore, a successful outcome with limited or no evidence of self-confidence or self-motivation. Perhaps they proved their own point? Now, if you wouldn't mind, we are curious which trait your group thought was absolutely essential in your ideal CEO?"*

"Take it away, Robin," Glenn volunteered. She made her way forward.

"We also found this task rather challenging. However, we did have unanimous agreement. We agreed that none of it would work if the person at the top didn't have a sense of humor." The class cheered; it was obvious there was agreement with her selection.

Each group voiced their conclusion. There were a variety of traits selected that the groups felt were not essential in order for a CEO to lead successfully. The justification for elimination was usually anchored in the belief that the benefit of a given trait could be purchased within the character of another employee. This trait would then be available to the CEO as needed. For example, vision could be purchased in the form of a futurist. Creativity in its various forms may be found in local artists. Intelligence could be sub-contracted from the regional university by utilizing its resources in research and development. Integrity was viewed as a by-product of a successful administration, much like confidence and motivation. Trustworthiness also fell under this justification. Effective communication could be accomplished by having the right assistant or wellgroomed public relations office.

As the discussion continued, it became apparent that many students felt current CEOs were in fact being protected by having good people running interference for them. Several examples were cited of prominent CEOs and officials who were once held in high esteem and only revealed at the bewitching hour as the corruption, fraud, embezzlement, and incompetence were revealed prior to some form of investigation or bankruptcy.

Desirable personal characteristics in the form of charismatic optimism and moral crusades were frequently revealed as shams or counterfeit imitations of uncontrollable narcissism. The conversation relating to trustfulness in personal or professional relationships began to suggest these traits no longer existed. It was time for me to step in. *"Let us shift our focus from those desirable but expendable traits to the one trait that virtually every group identified as the essential trait of an effective CEO: a sense of humor. When we get back from our break, we will discuss this elusive trait. However, before you go, I would like everyone to take a scrap of paper, borrow from your neighbor if necessary, and rate what you consider your sense of humor to be using a one-to-ten scale, with one being low and ten being high. Please drop that on my desk on your way out. Take fifteen; you deserve it."*

SECTION 5

A SENSE OF HUMOR

Unbeknownst to the students and certainly not what I had planned for the evening, we had drifted into an area of interest where I had considerable expertise and comfort. I have always been fascinated by the concepts of effective leaders and leadership and what makes them unique. A sense of humor is frequently cited as an essential trait, and I had invested considerable time and energy in my graduate studies chasing this elusive trait. It was now time to investigate some of the theories I had developed and get feedback from a vocal group. I was enjoying the evening immensely and sensed the students were also by the quality of the discussion in class as well as their interaction with each other during break. I suffered no guilt over my lack of focus, realizing everyone else who had scheduled a Monday night class was already home watching football. This was fun.

"Welcome back. Before you get settled in, I would ask that you would complete one more task. Please take another piece of paper, and if you are currently working or reflecting on a previous boss, evaluate that person's sense of humor utilizing the same one-to-ten scale you used to evaluate yourself. Please pass your scores to the right, and Kim, would you please total these and calculate an average for us?"

"While you were on break, I had the opportunity to calculate the class average. I'm curious, what do you think it was?" The responses ranged from a low of four to a high of nine.

"Survey says, seven point zero." I reported. *"Now Kim, what did our bosses average?"*

"Survey says, three point seven five." A big gasp from the class was evident.

"There you have it. We tend to rate ourselves very high and those we work for very low. Psychologists would say this is a protective measure on our part because psychologically it would be very damaging to our self-esteem if we concluded we were very low on the scale, or without a sense of humor."

"First of all, let me say your results are very similar to a variety of audiences surveyed before. First let me ask, was this a difficult decision for anyone, evaluating either your or your boss' sense of humor?" They all agreed it was not a problem.

"Secondly, what criteria did you use to determine your scores?" Silence prevailed. *"Think about this. If you were requested to estimate weight, height, or even IQ, you would have an established frame of reference or scale of some sort. Let's look at the other senses. Whether it is sight, smell, taste, touch, or hearing, we have instruments to measure it to a one minute decibel. And yet, we are quick to evaluate ourselves and others in reference to a sense of humor with no tangible base of reference. Why is that?"* I did not wait for a response. I knew it was not forthcoming.

"This is the question that is rarely asked and never resolved, and yet understanding this trait lies at the very foundation of comprehending leadership. Not only is it critical to one's professional success, it is the number one characteristic desired by both men and women in a significant other. And we don't agree on that much.

Let's first ask the question, is it truly a 'sense' in the purest form? If we consult Webster, sense is defined as 'a bodily function or mechanism involving the action and effect of a stimulus on a sense organ.' If we consider a sense of humor in context with the other senses, the inconsistency jumps out. It is easy to identify the sense organ associated with any of the other senses: sight, smell, taste, hearing and feel/touch. And the organ associated with humor? Non-existent. In short, it is a stretch to identify humor as a sense at all."

"However, let's not get hung up on the semantics and whether or not it is a sense. Let's just talk about what it is. So please, I know you have some opinions. You tell me what it is, and I'll do my best to capture your thoughts on the board. Who's first?"

"Well, it's kind of hard to explain. It's one of those things, you know it when you see it," was the first contribution.

"Okay, what I'm hearing is, it's mysterious and subjective." I listed those on the board.

"Yea, it's like success. You know it when you see it," he offered.

Another student jumped in. "Hang on. I don't think success is mysterious or subjective. Show me your checkbook, and I'll tell you on the spot if you are successful." We all laughed.

"Is there anyone in here who doesn't think Bill Gates is successful?" I asked.

"I'm not sure," was a voice from the back.

"And you are?" I inquired.

"MaryAnn Jacobs," she responded.

"Okay, Miss Jacobs. Why do you hesitate to acknowledge Bill Gates as a success?" I asked.

"Well, because we really don't know who Bill Gates is. We know he's good at making money and he appears to be pretty smart, but we don't know who he is behind closed doors. And I think that's more important in determining if someone is a success or not." Applause from the class rang out.

"It sounds like you have some supporters here, Miss Jacobs," I offered.

"Well, thank you. I need all the help I can get," she responded with a laugh.

"I'm hearing support for both mysterious and subjective. Is there another descriptive word that defines what a sense of humor is? Is success in some form a prerequisite for a sense of humor? Before we move on, let's define success. If you don't mind, young man, reach your left arm out and grab that dictionary sitting on the bookcase and let us know how success is defined.

"Will do, and my name is Rick Myers in the event you are recording extra credit points," he gained class support as he began flipping pages.

"Here we go, success; a favorable or desired outcome. Second definition of success is the gaining of wealth and fame."

"According to this definition, Bill Gates certainly deserves the designation of success on both accounts. How about Mother Teresa? Does she qualify as a success?

A resounding yes from the class. "She certainly had the fame." I observed. "Did she have a sense of humor?" The lack of response was indicative that none of us felt comfortable with attaching the label of humor to Mother Teresa because of our limited exposure to her.

"So, what's the consensus? Is humor, as we have defined it, a characteristic of success?"

"No, absolutely not!" "There are too many examples of people with a great sense of humor that are neither wealthy nor famous," were the responses.

"So let's refocus. In addition to being mysterious and subjective and not necessarily reserved for 'successful' people, what other descriptive words do we have to define this desirable trait? Note, I didn't call it a sense," I offered.

"It makes you feel better when you are around them. I'm not sure what you would call that?"

"Contagious?"

"Thank you, Carol. Is there agreement with this? Should I add it to the list?" The class offered *u*nanimous support.

"To me a certain irony exists here. We have identified that the most desirable trait in a CEO or a leader or in a significant other is a sense of humor. We have further clarified that it truly is not a 'sense' at all, and the best description we can come up with is that this desirable trait is mysterious, subjective, and contagious. A rather soft definition if you ask me, and yet, we are very quick to evaluate to what extent or degree this trait is present not only in ourselves but others as well."

"Here is your assignment for next week. First, I would like you to pick up a syllabus for next week on your way out. Please note the required textbook listed and the reading assignment."

"Also for next week. Obviously, we have given a lot of weight or credibility to the importance or significance of a sense of humor as it relates to leadership and by inference, upward mobility. I would like you to bring in anecdotal examples of 'successful' people displaying humor. Secondly, bring two contributions from credible sources that would either support or refute this elevated status we have granted to humor."

* * *

"Welcome back. I trust you had a good and prosperous week. I was pleased from the message I received from the registrar's office that no one dropped the class and that we have added a few to max out the enrollment. To those brave souls joining us tonight, I offer a warm welcome. I would also remind you that the opportunity to drop or add a class ends this Wednesday, in the event you may have overlooked the fact that this class does take place during Monday night football." Some feigned disappointment and scooted their chairs as if they were going to exit which generated a chuckle from the class.

"All right, don't say I didn't warn you. My name is Jim Haviland and the class is entitled, Emerging Patterns of Leadership. Here is the syllabus, which has provided very little guidance, if last week is any indication. Please raise your hand if you need one, and we will be underway."

I continued. "In an effort to bring you up to date, we became a little side tracked trying to identify why some leaders or CEOs were paid in excess of $400 an hour, I believe, calculated by Mr. Wright by dividing $1,000,000 by the standard 2080, the number of work hours in a year, given a forty-hour work week. We concluded CEOs possessed some personality traits that may justify this generous salary. Now class, help me out; you say the desired trait, and I will list them on the board again." The students called them out one at a time.

"After considerable discussion, we concluded that many of these traits may possibly be provided by other key staff members, but the one trait that is absolutely essential for success and incidentally the same trait we seek in a significant other and that is? Help me out, class."

"A sense of humor," was delivered in unison.

"We then made two other significant findings. One, that a sense of humor is essentially not a 'sense' in its purest form, unlike the other 'senses' linked to a particular body organism, like a sense of taste would be associated with the tongue. Secondly, we concluded, it is difficult to pin *down precisely what a sense of humor was, although we know it when we see it. Then, much to our embarrassment, we realized we were quick to rate ourselves and others on a one-to-ten rating scale, the degree to which this trait was present, although admittedly the trait was mysterious, subjective, and contagious."*

"So in short, you didn't miss a thing." Laughter throughout the class. "Oh and one more thing," I added. *"We concluded that success in our culture was defined by wealth and fame, although we recognized that it was possible to be considered successful without acquiring wealth or fame."*

"What would be an example of that, where success was achieved without those outcomes?" One of the new students asked.

"Let's see. I think we referred to Mother Teresa. However, she did achieve fame, and it could be argued that innocuous lottery-winners would be considered successful by most people, but hang on; it may simply be the fact that they have now achieved fame that makes them 'successful'." I was struggling for clarification.

"I know. Take a parent or couple who have who have raised a good child or family. I think most people would identify that achievement as 'successful,' and yet there is no wealth or fame attached to it."

"Now that I think of it, it makes you wonder, is that why so many people have kids? Is raising a good family one of the more commonly and readily acceptable ways of obtaining success, but not necessarily achieving wealth and fame?"

"In any event, I have asked that you bring in examples of humor demonstrated by 'successful' people and also some definitions of leaders or leadership which will be shared later. However, prior to that, I would like to confuse the issue even more.

Therefore, does it confuse the issue if I say, be aware that humor has little to do with jokes or comedy?" Mass confusion and looks of perplexity prevailed.

"Let me explain," I urged. *"I had the opportunity to consult William Funk's work, Word Origins and Their Romantic Stories. According to Funk, we borrow the term 'humour' bodily from the Latin. Ancient philosophers believed that the mixture of four fluids within our bodies was essential to determining one's health. (Much like today's blood sample reveals so much of what is happening internally.) The mixture, color and*

texture of blood, phlegm, bile, and black bile were the key to determining one's health. So how does this relate to one's sense of humor? It may simply be a matter of convenience and evolution of terms regarding the merger of two dynamics. The Latin word for liquid is 'humor,' and the Latin word for mixture is 'temperamentum'. In short, if the mixture (temperamentum) of these four liquids (humors) was satisfactory in color and texture, one was considered healthy or to have a humorous temperament. Please note having a humorous temperament has nothing to do with jokes, one's ability to tell jokes, or comedy. It has to do with being healthy, and it doesn't stretch one's imagination much to see how other behaviors consistent with a humorous temperament like smiling, laughing, and likeability would over time be associated with jokes and comedy. Humor has nothing to do with jokes and comedy."

"It is a disposition, and acknowledging it in this form explains why it is so mysterious and subjective in nature. It also explains why it is contagious. We have a tendency to smile back at those smiling at us, and we have all witnessed how one infectious laugh may spread throughout an entire theatre.

"So let me recap. We have determined that a sense of humor is a desirable trait. We have also concluded that this trait is not a 'sense' in the purest form, and now we have the revelation that it has nothing to do with jokes or comedy as commonly believed. So how are we doing?"

"What was the ending date for that 'drop-add period' you mentioned?" A brave soul ventured much to the enjoyment of the rest of the class.

"So, with that being said, who would like to share their anecdotal example of humor? I challenged.

"I'll give it a shot," student Mike Ridgeway offered. "When Lee Iacocca, a non-candidate for President, was constantly badgered by the press regarding the possibility of a potential candidacy, he quipped, 'I have no political ambitions and would appreciate a different line of questioning.' He added further clarification, 'I find that line of questioning tiresome, and besides, it makes my campaign manager nervous.' The magazine article states the room erupted in laughter."

"I'll go," Mary Ann jumped in. "When Senator Douglas accused Abe Lincoln of being a hypocrite, wishy-washy, and two-faced, Lincoln won the crowd over by declaring; 'I've just been accused of being two-faced. Now I ask you, if I had two faces, would I pick this one?' We all know the end result."

"My turn, here's one I heard the other night."

"A man was driving down the street in a sweat because he had an important meeting and couldn't find parking. Looking up toward heaven, he said, 'Lord, take pity on me. If you find me a parking space, I will go to church every Sunday for the rest of my life and give up drinking.' Miraculously, a parking space appeared. The man looked up again and said, 'Never mind. I found one.'" Good response from the class. More moans than not.

Glenn Wright got philosophical on us. "I looked up jokes at the library and came up with this. The bride was disappointed when introduced to the prospective groom. 'Why have you brought me here?' she asked reproachfully. 'He's ugly and old, he squints and has bad teeth and bleary eyes …' 'You needn't lower your voice,' interrupted the broker. He's deaf as well." Moans throughout the room.

He continued, "That was taken from Sigmund Freud's work, Jokes and the Unconscious. I must admit I found the book rather fascinating, before I got in over my head. If I understood what he was saying, man experiences conflict as he simultaneously seeks pleasure while avoiding criticism. Jokes provide a release from that tension by providing an avenue to experience the desired pleasure and limit the possibility of criticism.

"I quit reading when the topic of alcohol was introduced, because I was going out later. Apparently, alcohol reduces the inhibiting forces, criticism among them, and makes pleasure more accessible. Two other things, if I may? Freud did quote a guy, Lipps? He agreed with what we had said in class about humor being totally subjective. I found the discussion about how both conflict and tension coexist, and humor provides a release value very interesting. I mean, how many times have we heard somebody say, 'It was just a joke,' as justification when somebody takes offense? I recalled how ballistic that comedian from the Seinfeld show acted by increasing racial slurs in his act even when the racially-mixed audience wasn't buying into his material. It made me realize how closely related humor or jokes may be to hostility or aggression."

I contributed. "I do believe Freud went on to say, that which we laugh at the loudest may be an indication of where our personal tension or *aggression may be the most intense. For example, someone who resents his boss may laugh the loudest at the joke, 'My boss' definition of long-range planning is where to go for lunch.' And we all have seen 'straights' laugh hilariously at 'gay' jokes. I believe Freud would suggest, what lies at the unconscious level may be far more revealing than we would like to think."*

"Thanks, Glenn. That was great." I complimented.

"One more thing, Dr. Haviland, if I may?"

"Surely," I responded.

"I hate that when people call me Shirley," (cheap, but thoroughly enjoyed by all of us).

"Yes, Mr. Wright. What would you like to add?"

"I just had an epiphany," he declared.

"Please share," I encouraged.

"When Freud said we would seek pleasure and avoid criticism, he was right. In the form of confession, I would like to admit in my earlier joke about the wedding couple; I switched the joke to be on the bridegroom rather than on the bride. Why? When I anticipated telling the joke tonight in class, I thought there might be criticism if the victim were the bride and not the groom, as I told it. I wanted the pleasure of telling the joke but avoiding any possible criticism. I think that Freud guy may have been a pretty bright guy."

Applause and laughter.

"He had his moments," I agreed.

As the commotion died, "On that note, I should jump in. As the son of a preacher man, I know I've heard all of the jokes," he said jokingly. "When I mentioned our assignment to my father, the preacher, he referenced a book by Eldon Trueblood, The Humor of Christ."

"I told him I wasn't aware of any examples of humor by Christ. He said, most people weren't, but it can be found in the parables. When Christ made reference to the unlikelihood of a camel getting through the eye of a needle, it would be analogous to a contemporary speaker referring to a snowball's chance in hell."

Interesting perspective. When indications or examples of humor are taken out of context or aided by the distortions of time, the impact is lost. I don't imagine the insertion of "Where's the beef?" would get much response from a contemporary audience. However, this quote from a very popular Wendy's Restaurant commercial was pivotal when delivered by candidate Walter Mondale and directed toward candidate Gary Hart.

Freud also referred to this, indicating most jokes have a timely topicality and are frequently dependent upon a wide variety of experiences and exposure. I'm reminded of the quips Bush Sr. made when running against Michael Dukakis when he said,

"*Dukakis's foreign affairs experience amounts to eating breakfast once at the International House of Pancakes,*" in addition to his line, "*Dukakis thinks a foreign market is a place where you go to buy French bread.*" In order to completely enjoy that line, a certain degree of exposure would be desirable opposed to offering a 'knock-knock' joke.

This dependency on exposure and timeliness may explain a degree of sophistication necessary to appreciate some jokes and double meanings offered by comedians. It certainly would explain why some elderly people may appear to be humorless. It may simply be the fact that isolation from worldly events may be the true culprit.

"*I have a political example also,*" offered another student. "*When John F. Kennedy was running against Hubert Humphrey, he said, 'Hubert's problem is that he has too many ideas and too much energy. He alarms the country. I think the people want a less controversial and more boring candidate, someone like me.*'

"*According to Gerald Gardner, author of All the Presidents' Wit, 'it's a toss-up between Kennedy and Reagan. Both have been very adroit in using humor to ingratiate themselves and to defuse sensitive issues. Kennedy was willing to make fun of his Catholicism, wealth, and inexperience as he pursued the highest office in the land.'*"

"*I found an interesting one. In Mark McCormick's book, What They Didn't Teach You at Harvard Business School, he cites a sense of humor as the second most important trait necessary for success. The first? Common sense.*"

Following contributions from about fifty percent of the class, I abruptly inserted, "*So what do you think? Did we hear some good examples of humor in action?* Most nodded approvingly.

"*I don't think so,*" offered one of the newly added students.

"*And you would be?*" I asked.

"Marcie Grimes."

"Okay, Miss Grimes. Tell us what you're thinking," I encouraged.

"Well, if I understand what you said earlier, humor is a disposition and what we have just heard are jokes or examples of comedy."

"Bingo." I responded. "You're right on target. Now, if the response from Lincoln regarding his two faces was an off-the-cuff original, which it may have been, it would be considered a spontaneous and non-defensive remark, therefore indicative of his disposition. On the other hand, if his response is part of his scripted repertoire relating to his flip-flop on issues, it would be considered a joke or attempt at comedy. There is a big difference, one being a sincere reflection of disposition, the other, a sound bite of who the man wants you to think he is. It's very hard to distinguish between the two given an isolated example because the lack of sincerity may be camouflaged in its delivery." A pause to allow for reflection.

"Not to confuse the issue even more, but frequently the desired end result, audience approval, may be the same regardless if it is a true reflection of the person's disposition or merely manipulation of the audience.

In an earlier life (many years ago), I worked celebrity security for the MGM Grand Hotel in Las Vegas. I remember standing side stage during Dean Martin's early show at 8:00 p.m. My only exposure to the man prior to this was via television like most people. I was aware of his reputation of being quite the drinker only by way of gossip and the mockery he made of himself in the skits he performed.

The truth is, he drank only orange juice before the show and then poured a glass of water with a twist of lime as he was being introduced. Upon introduction, he staggered unto the stage acting totally inebriated and disoriented. Midway he yelled out, "LOOK OUT!" pointing upward toward the single spotlight focused on him in a dark auditorium. "Oh my God, I thought it was a train." And it did look like that, and the audience roared. I remember saying to myself, "Boy, this guy is good, totally spontaneous."

I held that belief until approximately 10:05 p.m. that evening, when the second show began, complete with the twist of lime, the staggering walk and "LOOK OUT!" I remember I felt like a stooge. I felt I had been had. There wasn't one ounce of spontaneity in that entire performance. Every gesture, every raised eyebrow, and every belly-laugh, fully orchestrated and rehearsed. The fact that he was able to pull it off so well, night after night, was a testimony to his professionalism and also a lesson in life for me.

The 2008 presidential election provides some immediate examples of this dynamic. *"What is the difference between a hockey mom and a pit bull?"* A line delivered by Sarah Palin as she viewed hockey mom signs in front of her (pause); *"Lipstick."* And the crowd erupted in applause. I would suggest that was a scripted or coached line, a joke. However, the delivery was flawless and appeared spontaneous. It endeared her, possibly for a lifetime, to millions of Americans.

Mike Hucklebee received a similar bump in the polls during the primaries when asked, "What would Jesus do if he were in a similar situation?" And Mike responded (paraphrased), *"First of all, he wouldn't be stupid enough to run for public office."* Deafening laughter and applause from the class.

I believe by virtue of his body language and facial expression, he was caught totally off guard by the question, which made his response all the more impactful because it appeared spontaneous, unrehearsed, and unscripted.

His trip to the mountaintop was short lived. In the days immediately following the debates, it was obvious he thought he had struck a vein with the American voters and began inserting witticism at virtually every stump speech. *"He may not be able to part the Red Sea, but he was able to part the red tape in Washington."* The scripted and rehearsed one-liners came across as being insincere and ingenuous. It was the difference between evident spontaneous humor demonstrated in the debate and the canned predictability of rehearsed jokes.

John McCain's ill advised, *"Bomb, Bomb, Bomb Iran"* opening was another failed attempt to appear spontaneous by inserting scripted material orchestrated to get a laugh. These failed attempts frequently leave an audience perplexed trying to figure out who is the real person.

"Let's refocus with some more examples with one additional dimension. Let's try to evaluate the example and categorize it as either an example of humor or jokes and comedy. Better yet, let's get rid of that word comedy in the discussion, and we have Funk to thank for that explanation also. According to Wilfred Funk, the origin of the word comedy stems from

the Greece of two millenniums ago. A 'komos' was a festival. The chief singer at the festival, the Komoidos, eventually evolved to comedian, and we derive the word comedy. So give your example, and we will categorize in one of the two columns on the board. Is it evidence of humor or a joke?"

Virtually all the remaining examples were categorized as jokes opposed to true indications of humor. Ronald Reagan provided some interesting conversations with several examples of his wit offered as evidence of humor. Without a doubt, the favorite was his response to Walter Mondale's reference to Reagan's advanced age in the second debate. Reagan's response was; "I will not make age an issue in this campaign. I am not going to exploit, for political purposes, my opponent's youth and inexperience." Even Mondale laughed. However, more importantly, they never returned to the issue again.

Another telling comment coming from Reagan was his remark to the surgeons as he was placed on the operating table after being shot, *"I hope you're all Republicans."* We have no way of knowing if the age response was rehearsed; one would suspect so. However, it is highly unlikely that the comment in the operating room was rehearsed given the timing and the immediacy of the action. Ronald Reagan ended his term of office with the highest approval rating of any president since Franklin Roosevelt.

The irony is that Reagan received negative ratings for his handling of every social issue posted: civil rights; 51 percent negative, education; 54 percent negative, housing; 65 percent negative, and welfare; 67 percent negative. On the other hand, the same survey noted two-thirds of the responses rated his leadership ability as excellent or good. Three-quarters favorably rated his charisma and ability to communicate.

Many students chose Reagan as their selected example of one demonstrating an effective use of humor. Perhaps that contributed to Reagan being recognized as "The Great Communicator." Reagan was also a dedicated student in the study of Abraham Lincoln, another successful individual who was frequently cited as possessing a keen sense of humor.

One of my favorite comments about Iacocca was offered by Peter Wyden in his biography of Iacocca, who was making the equivalent of $8,653.85 per hour at the height of his career ($17.9 million annually) with Chrysler. Incidentally, when Iacocca was confronted by the press when his substantial salary was revealed, he responded, *"I was embarrassed,"* he said. *"But what should I do? Should I root for the stock to go down?"*

In reference to Reagan, Iacocca states, *"You know, in life there are some people you meet whom you'd just like to pal around with. They're fun, they put you in a good frame of mind, and they make you feel terrific. Well, that's Ronald Reagan."* Iacocca later adds, *"There's no way on earth you could dislike him."*

Following the break, the balance of the evening was consumed by sharing various definitions of leadership that had been found from over 600 definitions available, according to Burns. The class favorite was, *"Leadership is the ability to be out of control comfortably."*

It had been a most stimulating evening. *"Next week, we will scrutinize this critical trait more closely. We will examine not only the origins of humor, or should I say a humorous disposition, but the value of this disposition as it relates to leadership. We will examine what happens to it and how one may regain it. Keep up with your reading, and have a good week."*

* * *

"Well, welcome back. I trust everyone had a good week, and we welcome the new students who have joined us during the drop and add period. I am Jim Haviland, the instructor of this class entitled 'Emerging Patterns of Leadership,' and I am the one responsible for leading this class on a wild goose chase over the past few weeks."

"Allow me to bring you up to date. We began discussing why it is that some people make so much more money than others with apparently the same qualifications. We concluded it was due to personality, and then went on to document some of Carnegie's work that states as much as 85% of one's success directly attributed to one's personality, regardless of the occupation."

"Incidentally, class, I think you will find something similar to this finding in Malcolm Gladwell's recent book, Blink. He presents the case of an insurance company seeking to find out who, among all the physicians covered by the company, is most likely to be sued for malpractice. What they found out was the risk of being sued had very little to do with how many

mistakes a doctor makes. The major factor that influenced whether or not a suit was initiated was how the patient was treated on a personal level by their doctor. The difference was entirely in how they talked to their patients. Again we are back to personality, and the medical community just happens to have another word for personality as it applies to physicians: bedside manner. We went on to identify several traits consistent with leadership such as charisma, self-confidence, etc. and then did a forced choice to determine which of these traits are not essential, primarily because they can be found in competent assistants. These traits range from intelligence to creativity. However, we concluded that a sense of humor was critical for success at the executive level."

"*We then rated ourselves on a one to ten scale, with ten being the highest, what we perceived our own sense of humor to be. And the class average was?*"

"*Seven-point-five,*" the class chimed in.

"*And why was that significant, Marcie?*"

"*Because we then submitted what we perceived our bosses' humor to be, and it was much lower. I believe the average was right around four.*"

"*And why was that important?*" I inquired.

"*Because it demonstrated either we were rating ourselves too high, or it was just a coincidence that all of us had bosses that were losers. But more importantly, we discussed how willingly we evaluate both ourselves and others on a trait where no benchmark for accurate measurement exists. This was even more awkward when we realized all the other senses have finely tuned instrumentation for measuring the acuteness of them.*"

"*Excellent, Marcie.*"

"*Now, Mike perhaps you could elaborate on the balance of our discussion for the benefit of the new students?*"

"*Sure. We looked at the definitions of humor to find out that it had nothing to do with jokes or comedy but was a medical evaluation of one's overall health as a result of mixing bodily fluids, also known as humors in Latin or Greek. I'm not sure which one it was. It is really more of a disposition than it is a trait.*"

"*Any other definitions come to mind? Yes, Robin.*"

"*We defined success as a favorable or desired outcome and secondly as gaining wealth and fame.*"

"*And did that clear up the matter?*" I asked.

"No, it only made it more confusing," offered Kim.

"Why was that?" I asked.

"Because it was pointed out that many people are considered successful but have neither wealth nor fame. I believe the example was couples or individuals who have done a good job parenting would be considered successful, but little wealth or fame as a result."

"Did we elaborate on any other characteristics of this trait?" I led.

"We said it was mysterious, subjective, and contagious," offered Brittany.

"Can anyone think of any examples we cited as demonstrating this mysterious trait?"

I heard, *"Reagan, Lincoln, Christ, Iacocca, and Palin."*

"Anyone recall Iacocca's salary at the time he was getting all the favorable press?" I asked.

"Over eight thousand dollars an hour!" several students offered.

"Might be worth taking a look at what makes a guy worth that much." I suggested. *"By the way I saw my department chairman this week and told him our class had taken a detour from patterns of leadership to the most important trait of leadership, and he gave it his blessing. I thought you should know,"* I confessed.

"Okay, excellent review."

"Now let's pick up the discussion from there. And let me approach some of the new blood that has arrived tonight and has not been contaminated by our previous discussions. Young lady in the red, may I ask your name?"

"Chrystal Shannon," she volunteered.

"Miss Shannon. Where do you think this mysterious trait of humor comes from?

"I would guess one is born with it" she offered.

"Are you from a large family, Miss Shannon?" I asked.

"I have two brothers and a sister" she said.

"Not to be presumptuous, but may I assume they are all from the same parents?"

"You may," she responded

"And would you say you all have a similar sense of humor?"

"Absolutely not," she quickly responded.

"Really? If you had to rate them independently and also yourself on a one to ten scale, how would you rate them?

She paused and wrote down some numbers. *"As you indicated during the review, I would rate myself about an eight, my oldest brother a seven, my sister a four and my youngest brother a two and I'm being generous with that."* That got a good laugh from her classmates. I believe they could identify with the family dynamics.

"Has it always been that way?" I asked.

She hesitated. *"No, I don't think so. As a matter of fact, I think we all got along well until my youngest brother hit middle school and he became a visitor from another planet."* We all laughed.

"So let's put this in perspective," I suggested. *"You indicated you came from the same parents; you believe each individual was born with a sense of humor intact, and yet there is a large range in your scoring of your siblings' humor, with you rating yourself the highest. Is that correct?"*

"Yea, but I don't like the way it sounds when you say it." Laughter. *"I guess what I'm trying to say is, it seems we all have a genetic makeup that contributes to our overall sense of humor, but regardless of the similarity in genetic makeup something happens in the home environment that has a tremendous influence on the final disposition of each individual. For my brother, when he went to middle school, it seemed like the transition had more of an influence on him than our home environment including my parents."*

"Do you think it was the physical move to a new building or facility that had the impact, or the fact that he was confronted with the adjusting to a new peer group?" I queried.

"I would guess it had more to do with making new friends and the entire adjustment of changing classes every hour, trying to fit in with a much larger group, the pressure of competing for a place on the team and his first exposure to mixed dances and all the pressure that goes with that," she volunteered. *"Now I'm starting to feel guilty that I wasn't more patient with him during that period."* Laughter and a lot of head nods from classmates that could identify with what she had to say.

"Why should you feel guilty? You had to make the same adjustment?" I challenged.

"Yea, but I had my older brother who was already attending the middle school there to walk in with me every day. And I made the cheerleading squad within the first two weeks of school along with my best friend from

elementary school. And now that I think of it, we were both invited to the first social dance event, and my younger brother couldn't get up the nerve to ask a girl to go when he was there."

"What conclusions can you draw from these experiences that relate back to our discussion of humor?" I was searching.

"Although it appears to be a level playing field, and for the most part it probably is, as we are children growing up in the same home environment, however very early in our development, other factors begin to have as much, if not more influence than our own parents," Chrystal volunteered.

"Excellent observation and summation, Chrystal. And I think you will find a plethora of research in both psychology and sociology that will support the observations that you have made regarding the influence of the parents and the home environment as well as the peer group. Now combine the insecurities that come with a changing body and personality with the influences of birth order within a family and all the variables that affect the disposition of the parents as well as the other siblings in the home environment, and we begin to realize the complexities that contribute to what we commonly refer to as one's sense of humor or the existence of a humorous trait. Let's take a break," I offered.

"Dr. Haviland, before we do, I have one question," from Rick Myers. "Shoot," I responded. "This plethora thing, is that a good thing or a bad thing?" Explosive laughter from the class. I was pleased how this semester was shaping up. This was a group of bright and highly motivated students eager to learn. I couldn't wait to return from break.

Over break, I had the opportunity to reflect on two experiences I had earlier in my career as I began my quest to identify what makes one person so much more successful than another. Carnegie's work regarding the importance of personality had a huge impact on me, and then I was confronted with the dilemma similar to what I had just experienced in class. If two people from the same household had such differences in disposition and considerable research had identified the home environment and peer group as being critical influences, at what age did this transition begin to stifle what appeared to be a very spontaneous and creative disposition of a child? I found my answer.

SECTION 6

RISK/SELF-ESTEEM

During the first five years of my oldest son's life, I cherished his creative works of art, reassuring him that there may be dogs that have wheels and cars with wings. As he entered kindergarten, I eagerly examined his work every evening wanting to enjoy the learning process with him. Reflecting on his day, he shared that they had to draw a tree and then tell the class about their tree. He eagerly showed his tree. It was a multicolored tree with a variety of colored leaves in the foliage and similar colored leaves lying at the base of the tree, obviously representing a fall landscape.

When I asked what he said to explain his tree to the class, his pride disappeared, and he attempted to dismiss my question by indicating four other students had gone before him. I acknowledged that, however, but was persistent in wanting to hear his explanation of his tree. And then the truth came out. With lowered eyes and a quivering lip, he went on to explain that the first four students the teacher had called upon had very similar trees; they all had a straight trunk with a green tuft of leaves at the top, commonly referred to as the "lollipop" tree. And then she called on my son. He said he didn't do it. In our society we would rather say we didn't do it than to look different from the others. It's called conformity, and in a larger arena, it is called the process of socialization.

I had an opportunity to witness the extent of this socialization process later in the year. I was teaching a vacation Bible school class and had to teach a twenty minute lesson to three different age groups. There were elementary-age students in one group, middle and high school in a second group and adults in the third. I approached each group as if there were a camera in the back of the classroom and I was filming three takes with the same introduction lines in order to experience their reaction. I entered the room with the elementary kids and casually announced, "I need a volunteer." And total bedlam broke out as kids jockeyed for position vigorously waving their hands and screaming "Pick me, pick me," at the top of their voices, believing the closer their hands were to my face the more likely they were to be chosen. And tremendous disappointment echoed about as those left standing witnessed the selection of two energetic volunteers. Those not selected slowly shuffled back to their seats with heads bowed wondering how the world could be so cruel.

With the second group, "I need a volunteer" was met with a variety of expressions ranging from utter disgust to beady-eyed stare downs challenging me to dare pick them. Others had looks of total disengagement and degrees of boredom approaching imminent death. And there was no discernable movement in the room.

Now, with the adult class. "I need a volunteer." Somewhere and some time along this journey called life, adults have learned that the best way to remain invisible is to avoid eye contact. They immediately became fixated with something on their desk, floor, or sweater. It could have been a speck of dust, but they weren't about to look up until some other poor soul, presumably one less experienced in the ways of survival, was picked. As soon as that individual was picked, the speck of dust had magically vanished, and a look of interest and engagement prevailed.

I was amazed at the contrast. What happens to that child within us full of life, totally spontaneous, willing to enjoy and experience life at every opportunity? Does that child still live inside us, and if so, does it want to come out? How about our families, loved ones, and co-workers? Would they like to experience that part of our personality that has lain dormant and has done so possibly since kindergarten? What is it we are so afraid of, and why do we have this obsession with always being safe? And most importantly, how does this obsession with being safe affect our sense of humor? I shared these three experiences with the class and a vigorous discussion pursued.

There was general agreement among the class that it was inappropriate to volunteer for anything, and yet the class could not come up with one example when volunteering for something turned out to have negative consequences. On the other hand, there were several examples cited when volunteering turned out to have a very positive effect. The examples included a great date and hopefully an upcoming engagement as a result of volunteering to fill sand bags for flood victims. Another student received recognition and a spot on the evening news as a result of volunteer work at a nursing home in addition to part-time work. There were a variety of other examples, and the warning to avoid volunteering seems to have its basis in the military; however, no one was able to cite specifically how that originated.

There was also agreement that the parents had considerable influence in the atmosphere that exists in the home, and their behaviors set the mood and many of the beliefs that influence behaviors later in life. These behaviors may be as subtle as establishing the mood that exists at breakfast or whether the family even met for organized meals. Traditions around holidays are established by the parents in addition to a variety of accepted behaviors including language, allowance, snacks, bedtimes, phone usage, homework, friends, household chores, and the list goes on. All of this would have considerable influence on one's disposition or in context with our discussion, one's sense of humor.

"Dr. Haviland, it seems as if we all are in agreement that parents and the home environment are critical players in the development of this sixth sense. (We had come to an agreement that we would refer to this trait as a sense to facilitate conversation), but it also appears obvious that somewhere along the line the individual begins to establish beliefs and behaviors that are independent of his or her parents, and the uniqueness of the individual personality begins."

"Thank you, Glenn, very well stated. Let's take a look. The other characteristic that seems to jump out is our desire to be safe, avoid risk, and conform in order to fit in. Why is that so important to us as individuals? As young children, we seem to be totally oblivious to this need. We run about totally spontaneously and creative in every aspect, and yet as adults we are almost zombie-like in our behaviors, why?

"Yes sir, your name, please?"

"Gary Reynolds."

"Welcome, Gary. Let's hear what you have to say," I encouraged.

"I think the whole thing has to do with self-confidence. If we lack confidence, the last thing we want to do is venture out into the spotlight and take a risk that may result in our embarrassment."

"That makes sense. Therefore, when opportunity presents itself, we have a tendency, as a rule, to take the safe, secure, and more predictable route. Is that what you're saying?" I questioned.

"Right on," was his immediate response.

"Can you give me an example of that in your own life? I urged.

"How many do you want?" he asked.

"Give us one to work with would be fine. Perhaps a recent one."

"How does last week sound?" he needled.

"Go for it," I encouraged.

"Okay, I'll try to give you the condensed version," he volunteered.

"It all began my senior year in high school. We were playing our arch rival in football, and I managed to catch a pass while running out of bounds, hit the Gatorade table, and knocked over three of the opponents' cheerleaders in the process. When I saw it on tape, it looked rather impressive. But the real fireworks started when I looked up, and just like in the movies, time stood still as I was looking into the bluest eyes I'd ever seen. (Moans from the class). *Hold on, it gets better,"* he warned us.

"*I found out her name was Sylvia, and I had a picture of her from the football program, with cheerleaders included, hanging on my wall until last weekend, which is almost four years after the sideline crash. She came with her husband of three months to my cousin's wedding last week, and we physically met at the open bar. She said she remembered the high school incident vividly and had always hoped that I would give her a call for *a Coke, a date, or anything in between,*" Gary continued in dramatic fashion, much to the enjoyment of the class.

"*I'm not even sure how I responded to her, but I do remember a whole sequence of flashbacks as I reflected on how many times I had thought about making that bold call to her and never did. And now never will.*" Silence in the classroom.

"*Dr. Haviland, I consider myself to be a confident kind of guy. Why do you think I didn't have the courage to make that call?*"

SECTION 7

CRITICAL CHOICES

The previous question presented an opportunity that I had anticipated would occur sometime during this discussion; it has to do with one's apparent willingness to take risks in order to be the person we want to be. I had been exposed to the theory years before while working as a probation officer and later teaching criminal justice at Northern Michigan University in Marquette, Michigan. The foundation of the theory is found in the second half of a book entitled *The Psychology of Self-esteem* by Nathaniel Branden. I took liberties with his theories in order to outline it on the board for the current students and keep it in context with our discussion relating to humor. I presented the concept to the students.

I suspect Branden's down and dirty response to Gary's question, *"Why do you think I didn't make that call?"* would be *"Because you felt unworthy."* Branden would then go on to explain that underlying one's desire for security and safety is a deep seated feeling of being unworthy and incompetent.

Preceding the above mental sequence is a mental foundation that is rooted in emotion opposed to intellect. The below sequence is a precursor to the above progression continuing with a feeling of incompetence. The entire sequence of response and development exist in order to remain safe and secure and avoid challenge and risk.

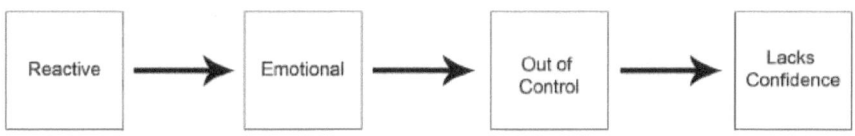

The entire progression from the initial stimulation at the bottom to the immobilization at the top due to the desire for security looks something like this:

I was interrupted at this point by Gary. *"It's amazing how much are desire to remain safe influences all that we do and say."*

"Well, stay with me," I encouraged, *"because when you see the option that was available to you it may make more sense. Branden would suggest there is another option (positive) that was also available to you given the identical circumstances. Bear in mind, this progression in both thinking and behavior appears to be spontaneous in any given situation; however in truth, the beliefs that govern the behaviors are well entrenched in the fiber of the personality and continually reinforced on a daily basis. In short, people who know you well can pretty much anticipate and predict your behavior in most circumstances."*

NEGATIVE	**POSITIVE**
Security	Risk
Safe	Challenge
Unworthy	Worthy
Incompetent	Competent
Lacks Confidence	Self Confident
Out of Control	In Control
Emotion	Intellect
Reactive	Active

Every decision is not a decision of **What to do**, but a decision of **Who you are!**

"The suggestion is, if one has progressed in one's development, keeping in mind the influences of the home environment, parents, peer group, and society in general along the positive vertical, perhaps that decision to ask Sylvia out would not have been so difficult," I offered.

Notice each undesirable trait (on the left) has a corresponding desirable trait on the right. As one progresses up the left scale they accumulate considerable baggage. Repeated daily and over a sequence of years, it is easy to understand how individual personalities become so apparent or obvious to others.

"*I had no idea that much thought went into the decision,*" Gary confessed.

"That's the irony. According to my understanding of Branden's work, the truth is probably very little thought went into your decision. You had a lifetime, in this instance probably sixteen or seventeen years, of being programmed to seek safety, security, and conformity since kindergarten. Therefore, in most situations, the less risky way is usually the chosen way.

Bear in mind, the catalyst for this decision is emotion, not intellect. This explanation goes a long way in explaining why it is that so many people end up living a life that is far less than what they imagined. They have a lifetime history of responding emotionally rather than intellectually to a variety of different opportunities in order to be safe, (and avoid risk); therefore they gain the security they desire.

Unfortunately, there are consequences that accompany this reaction. People end up marrying people they are not compatible with, stay in dead-end careers, have unwanted children, and the list goes on, in an effort to seek safety and security."

"*Why would having children provide safety and security?*" Jennifer asked.

I clarified the statement. "*I shouldn't have included that in the example. I think that applies more to the conformity or predictability that exist at a particular stage of life in order to fit in.*"

"*The way you explain it, or this guy Branden explains it, we have very little control over our lives because we have been programmed to respond a certain way, and for the most part an emotional way in most circumstances,*" Jason offered in a rather defeatist tone.

"*Quite the contrary,*" I responded.

"*Branden implies we are what we are as a result of the influences and experiences we have had. However, we have a choice as to where we go from here and therefore what we become and consequently, the life that we live,*" I went on to explain.

Most people look at life as a never-ending bombardment of situations that require decisions that must be made, and as we have discussed, for the most part respond emotionally in order to be safe and secure. Another way of stating the obvious is to do or choose to do what is necessary in order to avoid risk or change. There is a variety of research that addresses why people avoid risk and change. At the top of the list is that change involves uncertainty, and we are right back to our innate desire to remain safe. Change also provides an opportunity to fail, and to one who feels incompetent, the prospect of change borders on a death wish.

Another interesting dynamic in addition to the fear of failure that accompanies change is the fear of success which may be equally immobilizing. Imagine the guilt, the alienation, increased expectations, and loss of identity that success creates in one who feels unworthy. This observation goes a long way in explaining what appears to be the blatant course of self-destruction so many "overnight successes" seem to pursue. It is very difficult to be someone you feel unworthy to be.

Branden says rather than this never-ending succession of complex situations and decision-making, most situations may be reduced to one of three choices, which he refers to as volitions. In a given situation, we choose to:

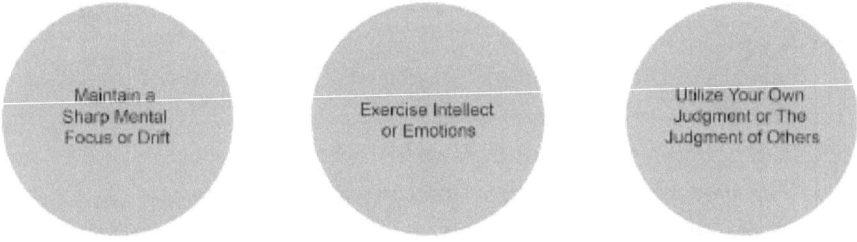

In reality, these three dynamics frequently overlap:

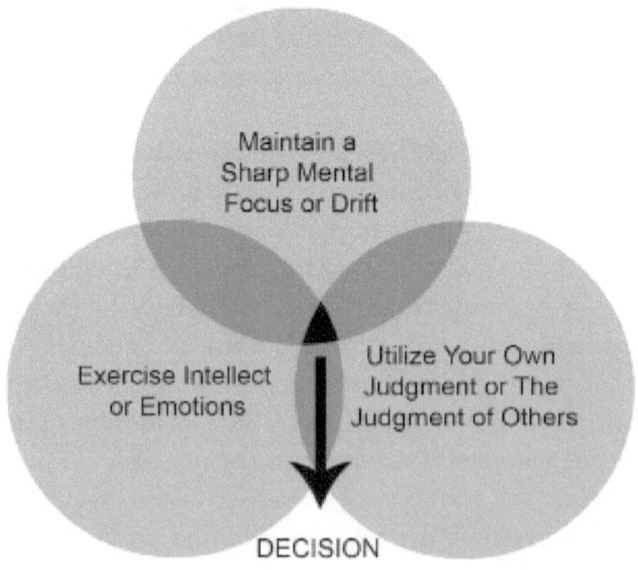

The Last Book ...

In essence, life is a series of situations, each of which requires a response. That response may be based on maintaining a sharp mental focus, exercising one's intellect, and utilizing one's own judgment, or one may drift, rely on emotional responses, and trust the judgment of others. Any given situation may be a combination of all three options or any one option.

"What would be an example of what you're talking about?" Reid asked.

"Well, let me ask, what will you do when this class ends tonight at 9:30, Reid?"

"I usually stop at the sports bar and watch the end of the Monday night game," he offered.

"And, what time will you get home? I inquired.

"About midnight, maybe 12:30 was his response.

The class chuckled, anticipating what was coming next. "Long game?" I questioned.

"Well, we have to diagnose and critique the game, ya know," explained Reid. More snickering from the class.

"What do you think Branden would say," I asked.

"Well, I'm guessing this guy Branden wouldn't be a big fan of football. Therefore, he would probably say I was existing in mental drift, being led by emotions and trusting the judgment or the influence of others over my own," was his response.

"I'm not sure, but out of curiosity, what are some of the rest of you doing after class that Branden might look on more favorably? I asked.

Some of the responses: "I go to work." "I have a guitar lesson." "I meet with a study group," and a variety of other responses that would be recorded on the positive side of the equation were offered.

"Wow, I'm starting to feel guilty. Is there ever any time to just kick back and relax? Reid asked.

"I would suspect that Branden would be very supportive of a relaxation break when appropriate, but I suspect most of us justify frequent and very long extended breaks with little regard for the time wasted, and more importantly, the opportunity to do something more constructive with our time. Now the more critical question may be how many of these extended breaks can one take before beginning to feel unworthy?"

There seems to be a great deal of consistency between what Branden is suggesting and the development of one's self-esteem.

"*Before we take a break, let's briefly circle back and tie this discussion relating to self-esteem back to an individual's humorous disposition. Any takers? Gary, I believe you were responsible for taking us on this ride. Any summary thoughts?*" I urged.

"*Sure. For openers, it seems like it would be totally inconsistent to think that an individual who possesses this desirable trait of humor could be one who feels out of control and lacks confidence. It appears that this desirable humorous disposition would develop if one consistently followed the course of positive choices, and probably impossible to achieve if one constantly followed one's emotional instinct,*" he offered.

"*Wow, pretty heavy stuff, Gary. You sure you want to stick with it?*" I asked.

"*Yea, I'm going to stick with it. And to think all I wanted was a date,*" he inserted.

And I jokingly responded, "*Isn't there anyone who will go out with Gary?*"

Much to my surprise, from the back of the room a very attractive coed responded, "*I will.*"

To which Gary responded, "*Are you for real?*"

And she responded, "*Sure, I'll give it a shot. I'm always good for a Starbuck's date.*"

"*You are on, my friend,*" Gary responded, and the class let out a huge cheer as we dismissed for break. It was a most interesting night.

When we returned from break, I resumed with the following, "*Over the break, I had an opportunity to meet with both Stephanie and Gary to be sure they didn't feel any pressure to commit to the Starbuck's date. For your information, both are fine with the commitment and plan to attend. However, this does present a teachable moment. Let's examine what just happened in context with our discussion of this evening.*

First of all, neither Gary nor Stephanie knows anyone else in the class. Why would that be important?" I asked.

"*I know,*" was an enthusiastic response from Brittany. "*When Gary put out the invitation, Stephanie accepted the offer, and then when Gary reciprocated, it would appear both had left themselves very vulnerable for* rejection. However, because neither of them knows anyone in the class, the influence of a peer group was minimized. What do you think?" she proudly announced.

"I think you're right on target," I responded. "Let's talk about the choices involved that would affect self-esteem." I urged. "Stephanie, if you wouldn't mind?" I invited.

"Go for it," she responded.

"Do you feel like you were maintaining a sharp mental focus during that exchange or drifting? Was my first question directed to Stephanie.

She responded, "Totally focused. I completely identified with his lost opportunity with Sylvia, as most of us probably do, but as I listened to him, I was thinking maybe she missed out on a pretty good opportunity."

"How about the other two dynamics? Were you exercising intellect or emotions and trusting your judgment or that of others?" I inquired.

"That's easy. Let me answer the second part first. Because I don't know another person in this room, the judgment was totally mine. And was it intellect or emotion? Perhaps some of each. From an intellectual standpoint, the truth is, I'm not asking the guy to marry me, I am just having a cup of coffee, I will meet him there, and I will have an escape plan, perhaps an expected call from home which I can't miss, to be utilized if necessary. And the emotional part, I like his dimples." Laughter erupted.

"And now for the Cash Cab question, what effect did that exchange have on their individual self-esteem and by inference, their humorous disposition?"

Unanimous agreement, "Both would be enhanced."

Rick Myers generated a new round of discussion by asking," Wow, when you isolate a particular example like Gary and Stephanie, it seems pretty obvious how their spontaneous willingness to take a risk is consistent with building confidence, but what would have happened if one of them would have said 'no thanks' to the date?"

"I don't know. What do you think, class?" I queried.

Marti offered, "Wouldn't it depend on how secure their confidence or self-esteem is at this point in life?"

"And what would determine that, Marti?" I asked.

"The experiences they had earlier in life that served to either reinforce a positive disposition or reinforce a negative disposition, according to what we said earlier," she responded.

"And if you had to guess, what would you guess their early experience would be, for the most part?" I asked.

"I would guess they had been positive for the most part," she volunteered.

"Why do you say that?" I asked.

"Because if their early experiences had been predominantly negative, they probably wouldn't have been so willing to risk rejection so publicly at this point of their lives."

Rick Myers jumped back in, "Yea, but he may turn out to be Jack-the-Ripper."

Strong head nods of support from the class.

"And that is precisely the type of mental argument that a more cautious person would entertain to justify not doing it and remaining safe. I suspect we could list two thousand reasons why Stephanie shouldn't do it, and they will range from every vampire movie, to Saw I, II, III and everything in between, to the brokendown car he may own to the possibility that he smokes and she doesn't. Any of these possibilities may serve as a good reason not to do it. For most people, there just needs to be one, one reason not to go, in order to justify remaining safe," I offered.

"And Branden is suggesting these parameters were set long ago; therefore, the possibility of even considering going is totally remote to a large segment of the population," Kim accurately clarified. "But the reality is Gary may be 'The One' for Stephanie, and if she doesn't go, she will never know."

Glenn Wright came to life, "Please help me. I'm exhausted. How many of these decisions do you think the average person would have to make in a lifetime, thousands, millions?"

"At one time I would have thought thousands during a lifetime, but I think this is part of Branden's message. We think we are these super complex beings in our thinking; however, the truth of the matter is we are so channeled in our mode of response, most decisions are already made internally, (or intuitively), prior to the situation occurring. Therefore, there really is no decision to be made. Furthermore, the people we associate with have a tendency to know what our response will be before they ask the question."

"The difficult or awkward situation occurs when we don't know how another will answer. If I may reflect back on our two dating examples, *what really prevented Gary from asking Sylvia out back in high school?"* I asked.

"Because he didn't know her, he didn't know how she would respond; therefore, he played it safe and didn't ask," Jason offered boldly.

"Exactly," I offered. *"How does that differ with what happened with Stephanie tonight? Jason, would you care to handle that?"*

"Well, first of all, he didn't really ask her. You asked if anyone was willing to go out with Gary. And when Stephanie answered 'yes' so quickly, Gary really didn't have the opportunity to think about it; he spontaneously agreed," Jason proudly stated.

"I'll accept that. Just reflect on the number of times you have initially wanted to do something, but you've overthought it and convinced yourself it may not be the 'safest' or most 'secure' choice; therefore, you had better not do it. This becomes the lament of older people when they reflect on lives that have proven to be less than fulfilling, 'If only I had'…"

"Before I forget, let me comment on the 'complex life' we think we live. I remember reading about the frequency of these 'emotional moments' we have during a lifetime. As I recall, the author cited, on average we have ten defining moments, seven critical choices and five pivotal people that have considerable influence on our lives. He goes on to say what appears to be a life of variety is frequently the same or similar experience being repeated. For example, if you dated but remained with that person due to a fear that you may not have anyone, has that really been a challenging experience or has that been a desire to remain secure? Now apply that same reason to the job you have and don't like but remain in it. Or consider the risk of going on vacation to add variety to life. Is it really that challenging if you go back to the same place repeatedly or is it again a desire to be safe? Something to think about until we meet again. Class dismissed."

As I sat in my study preparing for next week's class I continued to look at the abbreviated diagram of what we discussed in class the previous week. For convenience sake and to facilitate discussion within the class, we now refer to these three choices that are so instrumental in influencing one's self-esteem and ultimately humorous disposition as CB's or **"Critical Behaviors."** The progressions, positive or negative, that result from these critical behaviors are simply referred to as **"Consequences."**

CRITICAL BEHAVIORS

Positive: Focus/Intellect/Own Judgment
Active/Intellect/In-Control/Self-Confident/Competent/Worthy/Challenge/Risk

* * * * * * *

Negative: Drift/Emotions/Judgment of Others
Reactive/Emotion/Out-of-Control/Lacks Confidence/Incompetent/Unworthy/Safe/Security

Could it possibly be that simple? In many respects, it seems to be. Most of us can pinpoint those positive defining moments, critical choices, and pivotal people who have contributed to who we are. We can also identify those negative influences that have had a detrimental effect and have not assisted us in becoming the person we want to be. My experience has been that many people can isolate the exact date, time, and emotion that accompanied these influential events.

Unfortunately, the fact that one can identify these specific negative moments frequently provides one with an excuse or justification to continue in a less than desirable state. Therefore, we have a tendency to be reactive in nature, speaking and acting as if we have little control over these outside influences and subsequently view ourselves as unworthy. The older and more educated we become merely provides more experiences to support current behaviors, and we learn to articulate these excuses in a more convincing fashion.

I received a heavy dose of this helpless victim status as a probation worker and also later as I worked and taught in the field of criminal justice. I found very few individuals who had been convicted of crimes ranging from shoplifting to murder who felt any remorse or responsibility for their actions. And most were extremely articulate in identifying the outside influence that precipitated their actions. Perhaps Charles Sykes, author of A *Nation of Victims* said it best, "The chorus of powerlessness over one's problems has become so shrill that if Walt Whitman were to come back to America in the 20th century, he wouldn't hear America singing. He would hear America whining."

SECTION 8

EMOTIONAL TONES

During my doctoral studies relating to criminal justice and higher education, I came across a fascinating work by Ruth Minshull. In summary, it answered the question of how predictable people become in revealing their disposition, and they do it via one common denominator, emotion. Briefly stated, individuals manifest one of fifteen emotional tones, much like the easily identified tones in music. These emotional tones range from grim to great. According to Minshull, "Once we know the basic characteristics of each emotion, we can meet a person for the first time and, within minutes; we can understand his present frame of mind."

This intriguing concept became fascinating to me when reading the book, *Helter Skelter* which is the accounting of the Charles Manson murders. Manson has always been an enigma to those who work in the criminal justice field, not so much due to the celebrity of the victims but to the eagerness of the perpetrators to willingly kill at the direction of another person, Charles Manson.

In Part III of *Helter Skelter,* it implies that Manson was privy to the same knowledge base that Ruth Minshull later documented in her book entitled; *How To Choose Your People.* I found this connection to be captivating. If Minshull is correct, one well versed in recognizing the emotional tone of another may match that tone in order to befriend that person and subsequently rise above that tone in order to manipulate all tones below. As Minshull states it, "We will then know how well he's surviving and whether he will be an asset or a liability in our relationship." I would share this epiphany at the next class session, and the following exchange unfolded.

"Dr. Haviland, let me see if I'm keeping up with this conversation. You're saying that the one thing people have in common is emotion, and each of us gives off an emotional vibe that others pick up on, and if properly trained, one may become very sensitive to that tone, and if desired, may match that tone in order to develop a relationship?

In George Langelett's book, *How Do I Keep My Employees Motivated (2014)*, he refers to this as empathy-based management and defines it as real communication that occurs when we listen with understanding and respond in a way that honors the unique experience of others.

And this tone is most likely reflective of one's disposition, which we also associate with the trait of humor? Am I close?"

"You, Mike Ridgeway, are dead on." I applauded his insight. "I might add that is not as strange as it sounds, nor was Minshull the first to suggest such a phenomena. Some people attribute the same ability to animals, which explains a dog's overt reaction to some strangers but not others. Many of the horse whisperers and veterinarian types have been associated with a positive vibe that animals may sense."

"Dr. and Natalie Zunin entitled their book, Contact, The First Four Minutes, claiming four minutes is the average time, demonstrated by careful observation, during which strangers in a social situation interact before they decide to part or continue their encounter," I continued. "We can go way back to the pioneers in effective communication and find evidence of the same. Napoleon Hill is his seminal work, Law of Success, proclaimed the same type of personal connection was due to the vibration of bodily fluids that encompass all atomic matter. It sounds pretty sophisticated, but really it is another way of explaining why it is that when you can walk into a room of strangers you frequently get a sense of whose company you will enjoy and whom you would like to avoid. Where's that coming from?"

"Now the question becomes how valuable would that make you, if in fact people, felt that positive attraction emitting from you? Or in the parlance of 'business speak,' what would that make you worth to a company? I think we are starting to sense why this mysterious trait of a humorous disposition is so valuable," I offered.

"It reminds me of the credit card ad, 'It's priceless,'" offered Reid.

"Excuse me, Dr. Haviland, but a few of us were talking at break and came to the conclusion that it couldn't be this easy," stated newcomer Leroy.

"Elaborate for me, Leroy. What are we talking about, and what is so easy?" I requested.

"Well, if I understand this correctly, now that most of us are free from our parental, and for the most part our peer group influence, whether that be positive or negative, we are free to exercise our own CB's and make mentally sharp, intellectual choices independent of the judgments of others and create this humorous disposition that will be welcomed by all. Does that pretty much cover it?" He asked.

"First let me ask how thick your skin is? Or may I use this as a teaching moment?" I asked.

"It's as thick as an alligator, go for it," he urged.

"There are two issues here. First, Minshull would point out that emotional tones like to group with others of a like tone. Therefore, I assume those of you who were discussing the unlikelihood that it could all be that easy were in agreement?" I asked.

"That's true," he agreed.

"Can you see how awkward it would be for a classmate emitting a different tone to join in on the conversation? For instance, if someone were to approach the group with a very enthusiastic; 'Isn't this great to know how easy it is to take control of our lives?' I would assume they might receive a rather cool reception from your group?"

"Yea, I would say so," he agreed.

"Can you imagine another group in addition to your group, meeting in the same room during the same break?" I asked.

"Yes, I can. Okay, I get it. That would be an example of individuals seeking out a group emitting an alternative tone, a tone totally different than the tone of our group?"

"Precisely," I responded. *Now let's take a look at the tone of your group. Given your limited knowledge of Minshull's tones and the specific labels she attached to her tones, how would you describe the tone of your group overall?"* I asked.

"Well, I would say that we are skeptical and have a hard time believing one can take control of their life that easily," he offered.

I responded, *"At what point did I, speaking on behalf of Brandon and Minshull, ever indicate that it would be easy?"*

"In retrospect, I don't think you did. I think the concepts make it sound easy," was his response.

I agreed, *"That's fair, but let's take a closer look at the tone that prevailed within your group at break. You indicated you were 'skeptical.' Do any other words come to mind, or if I pushed for an answer, do you really think people can change their disposition by merely changing their CB's?"* I urged.

His response, *"If you pushed for an answer, as much as I would like to believe, I would have to say no. Does that mean I flunk the class?"* We all had a good laugh, and I could understand their doubts. If it is that easy, why don't more people do it?

I picked up Minshull's book and began to read, *"Let's consult the source. From my reading I think I recognize the category or tone. Let me read and paraphrase excerpts from the text and you tell me if it captures the overall mood of the group."*

"This tone wants to hang on to the past and does not want to attach to new concepts, because if they do, it rids them of the opportunity to whine. Sometimes people group together on this tone, crying for sympathy and help while offering nothing in return. No solution, no contribution, no concession is ever enough." I continued, *"If you suggest a solution to one existing in this tone, she will dissolve in a puddle and tell you it's impossible. She doesn't expect to rid herself of the problem; she merely wanted to wallow in the horribleness of it all ... and she wanted company. No person of this tone accepts a simple solution, and one firmly entrenched in this tone doesn't accept any solution.* I questioned, *"Shall I continue?"*

"No thanks. I now realize my skin is not that thick, and I'm disbanding the group that met at break." We all laughed.

"Leroy, don't be too hard on you because Minshull warns us not to judge too quickly. A person may demonstrate a specific lower tone; however, their existence in that tone may be only temporary and strongly influenced by a variety of circumstances that are affecting that person at that time. However, before I provide everyone a convenient excuse for existing in a lower tone, Minshull cautions us to not be too forgiving, because if in fact a person has chosen to live in this lower tone, you as a higher-toned individual have one of three choices; either merge with this lower tone in order to fit in, or flee from their influence out of self-preservation or temporarily match their tone in anticipation of bringing them up scale."

I added an additional caution to that, "Unfortunately, this is a trap too many people fall into. In their effort to assist another to come up on the tone scale (frequently referred to as an enabler), they sacrifice their own lives. This is the person who looks back and asks, 'Where did I go wrong?' or 'If I could only do it all over again.'"

"These group dynamics are fascinating. Let me give another example. We are all familiar with gossip, and most of us could label the individual going back as far as middle school who was the instigator of many of the rumors that circulated among our classmates. As we progress in life and enter different social settings whether it is high school, college, work, church or social groups of any type, we again can identify the person who assumes that role. However, in order for gossip or rumors to have wings, it must have an audience. The world is full of people who don't consider themselves to be 'gossips' but merely spectators listening to the gossip, and admittedly may pass along what they heard but only to their close friends. These individuals would be shocked and hurt if they were ever identified or included in the category of 'gossips.' Can you see the irony of this?" I asked.

"At the risk of going down another rat hole, I should mention in addition to Minshull warning us of this self-deception, Branden also tells us to take notice of this personality flaw. Branden refers to it as pseudo self-esteem; I refer to it as the imposter phenomenon. According to Branden, 'So intensely does a man feel the need of a positive view of himself, that he may evade, repress, distort his judgment, disintegrate his mind-in order to avoid coming face to face with facts that would affect his self-appraisal adversely. If and to the extent that men lack self-esteem, they feel driven to fake it.'"

I added, *"One can only wonder if this dynamic was at play when we evaluated our own sense of humor at an average of 7.5, and yet our boss or supervisor averaged 4.0. How humbling would it be if we asked our subordinates to evaluate us?"*

"Before we move on, I would like to elaborate on one other point that Leroy made which I agree with," I offered, and Leroy inserted, *"Please continue,"* which got a good chuckle from the class.

"It has to do with his observation that this concept of Branden's makes it too easy for one to gain control of one's life, and I would like to briefly address this based on an experience I had while living in Australia." This seemed like too good an opportunity to pass up an example of something both easy and beneficial to us, and yet we don't necessarily pursue it. *"I owned a health spa in Australia and spent a good portion of the day soliciting new memberships. Well, let me ask the relevant question to the class." "Please, by a show of hands, how many of you would like to be in better physical condition?"* Virtually every hand in the classroom went up. *"That's what I would have anticipated. Now the next question, who in here doesn't know how to do that?"* Not a hand in the air.

"And that, my friends, is the point to be made. We all know, and every prospect that walked into my spa knew, and knew from a very young age, it boils down to exercise and diet. No tricks, no gimmicks. It's just that simple. And yet, we live in an obese nation, with very few people unaware of what is necessary to get their bodies in the shape they desire. Now mind you, I'm not saying it will be easy, but it is necessary. Neither Branden nor Minshull said it would be easy, just necessary to make the appropriate choices. Instead, we invest in billions of dollars annually in pills and devices advertised on late night television hoping there will be some miracle drug, apparatus, or short cut that will enable us to avoid the obvious."

"Now please put this in context with our discussions relating back to a humorous disposition because the same principle applies. Humor is a trait that is extremely desirable, lucrative, and beneficial to us in both a personal and professional capacity. We know it is achievable if we make the right decisions, and yet few of us choose to. Therein lies why we admire and reward the few who have made the necessary sacrifice and truly possess this trait of humor. Let's take a break."

Following break, we began examining what gives a humorous disposition value.

"Dr. Haviland, right before break you were talking about how rare it is that one has a humorous disposition in spite of the fact the formula for achieving this disposition is relatively simple. Is the fact that it is so rare that makes it so valuable? I mean is it like the value of a rare painting?"

"That's part of it, Ted. If we just took the position that there are few people who really possess this trait that would probably make them more valuable than the rest of us. Aside from just being rare, what other characteristics does the trait suggest would exist, and why would that be valuable to an organization?" I asked.

Kim was first to respond. *"If we assume they have developed this disposition in conjunction with the appropriate CB's, there are a variety of good things that would emerge by definition."* I encouraged her to continue, *"For instance?"*

"Because of their confidence and willingness to accept challenges and take risk, I think they would create an exciting work atmosphere," she offered.

"Do you think this is the kind of atmosphere or boss that you would like to work for?" I asked.

"Absolutely," was her immediate response.

"As a rule, do you think this type of boss would be moody?" I inquired.

"I wouldn't think so," she volunteered

I immediately inserted, *"Perhaps this is what makes these people so valuable is the fact they are so predictable. Due to their confidence and willingness to take risk, they are approachable and receptive to people and their ideas, because they are not threatened. Now Ted, I'm coming back at you. What I'm suggesting is that trait that makes art so valuable, in addition to being rare, is the fact that people recognize it and therefore there is an element of comfort, similar to that of seeing a familiar face, opposed to seeing a stranger."*

"In some respects, the predictable and receptive nature of these people possessing a humorous disposition makes them approachable," I concluded. I couldn't help but have a flashback to an article I was reading last night. *Fortune* magazine selected Steve Jobs as the "CEO of the Decade." One of the articles interviewed eight people who rarely speak

publicly about Jobs. In an interview with Andrea Jung, Chairman and CEO of Avon and who sits on the Apple board, she states, *"There's an extraordinary openness in the boardroom. Any board member would feel free to challenge an idea or raise a concern. It's not only been gratifying; it's been great."* The article also addresses the simplicity of his approach, *"He (Jobs) makes it sound so simple, but he's taking on things that are extraordinarily complex and risky. He's laser-focused on getting it right."* Another reference to Jobs and consistent with our discussion relating to tones was made by journalist Michael Moritz, *"Steve's got a fabulous eye and a terrific ear. Most people in Silicon Valley or in the consumer electronics business are tone deaf, off-key. Steve has perfect pitch."* I'm sure Minshull would appreciate that metaphor.

"We can assume the opposite would be true?" asked Marti.

"Elaborate, please," I encouraged.

"Well, the person who does not possess this temperament would be one who is lacking in confidence, therefore struggling with feelings of incompetency, therefore seeking the safe and secure route, I would assume," she offered.

I challenged, *"What do you think their primary trait or characteristic would be in contrast to the predictable boss we just described?*

"I would assume they would be somewhat defensive and not very receptive to new ideas or risk," was her response.

I opened up to the class, *"Anyone ever had a boss like that?"* Virtually every hand in the class went up. *"Aha, a teachable moment. That explains two isolated facts we have addressed earlier. First, it explains why our bosses scored so low on our earlier survey rating them on a one-to-ten scale, and secondly, why people that possess the humorous disposition are so valuable to an organization. Because they are receptive to others and their ideas, they are capable of diffusing conflict before it dominates the organization."*

"Dr. Haviland, before we get going, could I share an experience I had this weekend that is textbook perfect for what we've been talking about?" This request was made by Jason who hadn't said much during the semester but seemed to be taking it all in.

I responded, *"Under one condition."* Does this have the potential to take us down another rat hole and dominate the discussion for the rest of the evening?" I asked.

"Yes, it has that potential," was his response, while the class cheered.

"Well, if that's the case, go for it!" I encouraged.

"To begin, I've been fascinated with these emotional tones we've been talking about, and I had the opportunity to see them in action this weekend. My uncle Bill won five tickets to the Vikings game on Sunday so he invited his three brothers and me. I'm sure my invitation was influenced by the fact I drive an SUV and willingly volunteered as the designated driver, which I was fine with.

"I picked Uncle Bill up first which allowed us a good thirty-five minutes prior to our next stop. Bill is a great guy, is doing very well as owner of his own business, and the Viking tickets were in recognition of a state sales contest which he had won. He was asking how graduate school was going for me, and we had a good conversation. I was telling him about this class and specifically about the emotional tones, which he thoroughly enjoyed. What struck me was how the mood and conversation changed as soon as my uncle Sid got in the car, and I think, because I had just been talking about the tones, it really caught my attention how the atmosphere within the car changed as we picked up each additional passenger. I began to listen very carefully to the contribution of each passenger during the four hour drive, and it was unreal how consistent they were in expressing a given tone regardless of the topic. The difference in tones was amazing given they were all raised in the same home environment."

"I think Ruth Minshull would be pleased with your observation," I encouraged him.

He continued, *"Now here's the big question. If I give you examples of their contributions to the conversation, will you be able to tell me their emotional tone?"*

"I'm sure Ruth would warn me not to bite on this with such limited exposure, but she's not here, so let's go for it. Allow me to get my resources in order." I removed her book, *How to Choose Your People,* from my briefcase. Jason removed his notes he had scribbled during the commute to the Vikings game.

"Great," he said. *"I made note of what they said regarding five different topics during the day in order to compare."*

"Wow, I sense we are at the entrance of a giant rat hole at this moment," I said. However, I wanted to continue due to his obvious enthusiasm

and copious notes, not to mention this was his initial contribution to the class.

"*Fire when ready,*" I commanded. *"No wait, let me set up a grid. You said there were four passengers in addition to yourself and you addressed four different topics. Is that correct?"* I asked.

"Yes, that is correct." I drew a 4 X 6 grid allowing for the four participants, their four responses and a place to identify the tone, if possible. Down the side I listed the uncles by name: Bill, Phil, Dick, and Sid. *"And the topics?"* I requested.

"I recorded their individual tone on four occasions: When they entered the car, opinion of the Vikings team, stopping at a rest stop, and when they were dropped off after the game," Jason volunteered.

We then began to fill in the chart according to what each uncle volunteered, and midway through the exercise as each uncle's emotional tone became obvious, students were yelling out in anticipation of what each uncle would contribute. The contributions from the class members, not privy to the conversation that took place during the drive, were amazingly consistent with what Jason had to offer. This proved to be a valuable teaching point regarding the consistency and predictability of a response once a tone is established.

We concluded the exercise by labeling the tone manifested along with some of the characteristics consistent with that tone. The completed chart:

TRIP TO VIKINGS GAME

Tone Scale	Characteristics of tone	Entering the car	The Vikings	Rest Stop	Departure
3.5 Interest Uncle Bill	Maintains interest and involvement. Inspires others/ Contagious	Ready to go. Concerned about me	"We are lucky to be seeing such a good team."	"That will be refreshing."	"Thanks so much for the game. Have a great week."
2.0 Antagonism Uncle Phil	Chip on the shoulder. Challenges & disagrees.	"How come you didn't pick me up first?"	"What's so great about winning a soft schedule?"	"If we stop it will just make us late. I say drive on."	"I expected a lot more. It wasn't one of their better games."
1.0 Fear Uncle Dick	Everything is dangerous. Postpones living.	Dressed for survival. "Be careful of deer, a good friend of his just …"	"If anything happens to Peterson the Vikings are done for the year."	"Is that the same rest stop where the girl was raped and kidnapped? I don't think she was ever found."	"Let me get my keys out first. You never know what can happen. A friend of mine…"
0.5 Grief Uncle Sid	Whiner/ victim clings to the past. Seeks pity, dependent. No simple solutions.	"I would have been ready, but my wife never…"	"They're just not like the 'Vikes' of '82"	"Try to park close so we don't have to walk."	"Great, home just in time to fold laundry."

This example also explains why we approach certain individuals given a specific topic and avoid others given the same topic. Although we may not have referred to them as emotional tones in the past, our subconscious mind has categorized them as such and we act accordingly to the best of our abilities.

A good example of this is evident in discussions relating to politics. We may never have had discussions with a peer regarding their political persuasion; however, we suspect what their views will be and offer opinions that we anticipate will be consistent with theirs in order to avoid conflict. When they blatantly demonstrate their party allegiance, we immediately make assumptions on how they will respond on a variety of issues.

My guess is most people consider themselves to be independent thinkers, and I am sure Branden would suggest this is in order to maintain a positive self-esteem; however, the pressure to conform to a "party line or position" may serve to influence one to a far greater degree than one would care to admit. This is never more evident than in Congress when critical issues require a vote. Put this is context with the CB's (critical behaviors) that have been discussed earlier, in particular regarding the importance of utilizing one's own judgment over the judgment of other's (party), and it is easy to empathize with those who hold elected offices and their desire to maintain high self-esteem.

Conflict takes place when one jumps or mixes tones and communication breaks down. By definition, individuals who exist high on the tone scale are individuals who hold themselves in high esteem, and the reverse of this is equally true; it is virtually impossible to have low self-esteem and exist high on the tone scale. We may temporarily be caught off guard when confronted with pseudo self-esteem. This dynamic exists when one does not conform to the perception we hold of them and their behaviors are totally inconsistent with our expectations; we feel we've been duped. We want individuals who hold high office and maintain celebrity status to be self-confident, self-assured, and consistently demonstrating a high tone. Unfortunately, the outer appearance may be in great conflict with the inner being, and we read about it in the headlines on a daily basis.

"Thank you, Jason for that contribution. Is there another rat hole we can crawl down this evening? Oh, wait, before I forget, Minshull also coaches us to be aware of some additional cues in detecting an individual's emotional tone:

How do you feel after talking with them?
How are they surviving?
Are they clearly understood?
What do they talk about?
Is the conversation shared equally between the two of you?
What is the frequency of accidents in their life?
What are they accomplishing?
How easily do they adjust to other tones?
What are their ethical standards?
What role do possessions play in their life?
Where is their orientation (past, present or future)?

"Hopefully, at this point in time, you will be able to discern what the desirable answers to the above questions are. If not, we may have a bigger problem. Here's an interesting question. How would Jason's four uncles respond to the eleven questions above given their grief, fear, and antagonistic tone of interest? Now, what's next?"

Todd raised his hand. "I've got one that has been bothering me since we met last time, and it's about Steve Jobs. I've always been a big fan of Jobs and I know he was responsible for 34,000 employees and increasing shareholder wealth by more than $150 billion dollars, but I never saw this humorous disposition that we have talked about."

"That's an excellent observation, and I'm surprised that it hasn't come up earlier. At this point, I'm not sure what Jobs' net worth was estimated to be. However, he is frequently seen as this stern and sober guy who maintained celebrity status among employees, customers, analysts, and rivals who scream as if he were a rock star when he walked on stage for a keynote event. So where is this humorous disposition that is so valuable? The truth be known, we are all making the same mistake in our assessment of Mr. Jobs. What is it?"

Jennifer took the bait. "We're measuring the wrong thing."

"Please explain," I urged.

"We are trying to project our own values and definitions of success on a person who thinks totally independently. From what I have read, he placed very little value on money, possessions, or celebrity status. I went back and read that article you had mentioned in Fortune magazine that declared him CEO of the Decade, complete with cover photo, the whole works, and yet he was not available to be interviewed for the cover story. Most celebrities would have died for that kind of exposure."

Another mistake is to think a sense of humor is demonstrated by a very outgoing personality, complete with abundant laughs and jokes. And if we think that, we are making the same mistake we mentioned the first night of class, and we now know humor has no relationship to jokes or comedy.

"What did you see in Jobs that would be consistent with a humorous disposition?" I asked.

"Well, with the exception of humor and charisma, it appears that he would have the ten remaining traits associated with leadership and our definition of success we identified the first night. His CB's couldn't be more on target, and that produced a very confident man who didn't shy away from challenge or risk. He didn't do anything to suggest he wanted to play it safe. Because we didn't see the man in public that much, it's more difficult to identify his tone. However, his success would certainly suggest he is high tone. I'm really impressed with his intense focus and how receptive he was to the ideas of others. I also think it's great that he was so dedicated to his family." Jennifer's insights were well received by the class.

"If these people are not motivated by the usual trappings of success, what motivates them?" Glenn asked.

SECTION 9

FLOW

The best explanation of what motivates people, if not the trappings of success, I've ever heard of is provided by psychologist Mihaly Csikszentmihalyi. He identifies a state of concentration that he calls "flow." This is a state so focused that it amounts to absolute absorption in an activity. The author states that many people may experience this while reading a great book; for him, it was while playing chess. Flow requires complete concentration to the task at hand, a task that requires utilizing the skills that one has to respond to a challenge that complements the skills at hand.

Recognizing that it is impossible to do justice to this enormous topic in these pages, I emailed Dr. Csikszentmihalyi seeking permission to include in this manuscript the diagram and explanation of *Flow* as presented in his book, *Good Business: Leadership, Flow and the Making of Meaning*. Within three minutes, he responded, "Sure, go ahead." I personally think this type of immediate response and willingness to share the intellectual property that he has worked years to create reflects volumes regarding what kind of a man he is. This type of unselfishness exists only at the very top on the "Tones" scale.

In reviewing his "Flow" diagram, some readers will interpret "Flow" as "Balance" within one's life. Maintaining a proper balance is the critical ingredient or foundation to happiness or contentment. Taking on too many challenges in life without a complementary skill set to accomplish these challenges will create anxiety in life. On the other hand, if one doesn't challenge the skill set they have, they will encounter boredom. Maintaining a balance is the secret, and this is when one experiences "Flow."

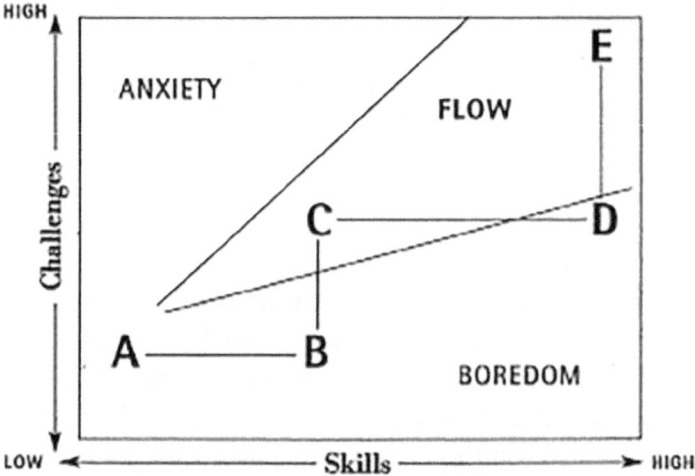

Figure 1: **Growth of Complexity Through Flow.** The flow experience occurs when both skills and challenges are high. A typical activity starts at A, with low challenges and skills. If one perseveres the skills will increase and the activity becomes boring(B). At that point, one will have to increase the challenges to return to flow (C). This cycle is repeated at higher levels of complexity through D and E. In a good flow activity these cycles can continue almost indefinitely.

In the words of Csikszentmihalyi: *"The ideal balance between challenges and skills never remains stable for long. Either one or the other component predominates, at which point adjustments will be necessary."* A conclusion that he makes as a result of research and speaking with successful businessmen similar to Steve Jobs: *"Contrary to common perception, there are many successful executives who understand that 'good business' involves more than making money, and who take the responsibility for making their firms an engine for enhancing the quality of life...The quality of the experience is the most important factor affecting overall satisfaction with life."*

Jason offered a summary statement, *"There seems to be a great deal of consistency for one demonstrating a humorous disposition, a high emotional tone, choosing positive critical behaviors, and now existing in an atmosphere of 'flow'."*

I concurred, *"It certainly appears that way. So now back to our decisive question. What would it be worth for an organization to have an individual at the helm who possesses these traits?"*

SECTION 10

CHANGE AVOIDANCE

"*Just before we go there, I have a concern,*" Gary Reynolds admitted. "*Let's just say, I wanted to ask a question for a friend of mind who couldn't be here tonight.*" Laughter from the class.

"Sure, Gary. What is it your friend wanted to ask?" I responded.

"*I have discussed what we've been talking about, and he thinks there may be room for him to possibly move up on the tone scale and perhaps develop the kind of confidence necessary for this flow to reveal a humorous disposition so desirable by others and organizations. Any tips you can give me to pass on to him?*" He was smiling now.

"I think so," I responded. "I'm sorry your friend couldn't make it, but who knows? Perhaps someone in class may benefit from the discussion, which may be long overdue."

"Sounds good to me," he said, as the class leaned forward and took out pen and paper.

I began. "The first step is to do a serious self-evaluation of why you want to change and how you would benefit if in fact you do change. Most people think the response to this is obvious; however, psychotherapists will warn that there are some risks and fears associated with change. Identifying the risk is usually enough to discourage any efforts related to change. Some *of the risks or fears we have alluded to before; however, let's briefly identify them once more."* I listed them on the board:

> **Risk and Change Avoidance**
> Involves Uncertainty
> May produce envy from friends
> May result in alienation from peers
> Presents an opportunity to succeed
> Requires action or decision
> May cause feelings of guilt
> May increase expectations
> Inconsistent with self-concept
> Opportunity to fail
> Coping with failure yields identity
> Unworthy
> Implies Change

"Change is a very interesting dynamic. I suspect that most people think that they have willingly adjusted to changes in life. However, I would submit that the majority of changes that have taken place in an individual's life are changes that have been necessary for survival, not necessarily improvement, and few have been made voluntarily. And there are good reasons why people don't willingly change. One of the primary reasons we resist change is that change is going to demand something from us, and we are not a generation known for our discipline or making sacrifices. We enjoy the comfort we have, and change introduces the unknown, and the unknown just happens to be one of our greatest fears," I continued.

"If we reflect back to the emotional tones scale, we know that 'fear' is one of the lower tones and frequently serves to immobilize an individual out of fear of what might happen. From a self-esteem perspective, to continue in a negative state may not necessarily be easier, but it is perceived to be safer.

Change introduces the fear of failure, i.e., one may not be able to make the change desired. If one currently exists at a lower tone, by definition one will have a lower self-esteem, therefore feel guilty about introducing change that is inconsistent with one's own self-evaluation, not to mention alienation from a peer group that may now experience envy due to one's improvement. Most peer groups will give lip-service approval to step outside the box, as long as you stay inside the circle."

"The whole thought of moving up in tone may be totally inconsistent with your own self-image, an image that has been created over a lifetime. One has adjusted to a life of failure; therefore, if one's image is altered with an improvement in self-esteem and tone, very likely there will be an increase in expectations placed on you. If success is felt to be undeserved, it will never be thoroughly enjoyed. We see this evidence of disillusionment in people in a variety of circumstances ranging from lottery winners to American Idol winners. Perhaps Austrian psychiatrist Alfred Adler said it best, 'How and to what extent we learn to overcome these feelings of inferiority largely determines our unique personality structure.'"

"Excuse me, Dr. Haviland. I think I'll just tell my friend who couldn't make it tonight he's better off just staying as he is," Gary responded, much to the delight of the class.

"Hold on, hold on. I can't leave you hanging like this, but it is important to note that change is not always easy, and people have a variety of reasons for not engaging in change. Let's treat the topic as if it falls into the good-news, bad-news category, and you have already heard the bad news. Is that okay? What do you think, Gary, would your friend be agreeable?"

"He would be tickled pink," was Gary's response.

"Alright, so let us assume we have completed our self-analysis and identified our shortcomings and come to the conclusion that the benefits derived from the necessary changes are worth the efforts necessary. Can I get an Amen to that?"

"Amen," was heard throughout the class. I walked to the board. "The first step is to identify which CB's (critical behaviors) are currently being exercised and subsequently affecting one's self-esteem, tone, and inability to experience flow,' not to mention influencing and demonstrating a humorous disposition. This step requires isolation of what you do with your time and in particular your free time."

The chart has five columns. The first column designates a time period, so I suggest starting at 7:00 p.m. on a Friday evening. For most people, this initiates a period of free choice that spans approximately sixty hours from 7:00 p.m. Friday to 7:00 a.m. Monday. Assuming twenty-one hours for sleep, there are thirty-nine hours that remain. This division of time reflects the typical nine-to-five forty-hour work week.

Adjust the time sequence on your chart to isolate the approximately fifty free hours that exist outside the work environment, allowing for sleep and mandatory commitments each week. Obviously, this distribution will vary for each person. Label the second column "Activity" and the third column "Critical Behavior." Record the activity that takes place during this time period and then identify each activity as positive (+) if it reflects sharp mental focus, intellect, and your own choice, or negative (-) if it reflects mental drift, emotional influence, or the choice of others. This will require a high degree of self-reflection and honesty to be a valuable tool.

I drew the chart on the board.

CRITICAL BEHAVIORS ACTIVITY SHEET

Time	Activity	Critical Behavior (+) or (-)	Tone (+) or (-)	Flow (+) or (-)
Friday 7:00-8:00				
8:00-9:00				
9:00-10:00				
10:00-11:00				
11:00-midnight				

The fourth column is labeled "tone," and the fifth column is labeled "flow." These two columns are subjective in nature; however, they serve to shed light on what is preventing one from being all one can be. Simply reflect on the activity that has taken place during the hour and ask, "Do I truly believe that activity would contribute to raising my tone and moving me closer to the 'Flow' experience? In consideration of tone, simply ask yourself, "Is this the type of activity that one who I aspire to be would engage?" If the response to the tone category is "yes," record a (+); if the response is "no," record a (-). With reference to 'Flow,' ask yourself, "Did the activity serve as a challenge to my existing skills or improve my health?" and record the appropriate response as yes (+) or no (-).

This exercise will allow for a lot of "Gamesmanship" to take place. One may easily justify watching three hours of television as "family bonding" if the children are in the room. I would suggest that an activity that requires an element of interaction with the children may warrant a positive score; however, watching television will be a stretch in most cases. It doesn't mean one can never watch television; just give it the score it deserves.

The tendency will be to assume progress is being made if a number of activities reflect a positive score, and this may be deceiving and serve to keep one constant with where one presently is in reference to self-esteem, tone, flow, and humorous disposition. I would encourage a minimum score of two-thirds of the scoring sheet be positive to indicate growth toward the desired goals.

"So once the selfevaluation and the CB chart have been completed, what's the next step?" asked Mary Ann Jacobs.

"First of all, the CB chart must be completed on several occasions in order to get a comprehensive view of how one's time is really invested. There will be a tendency to use the one weekend of the year when you help fill sand bags for flood victims as indicative of a typical weekend opposed to the three football game weekend," I offered.

"The real progress begins when you reverse the negative critical behaviors that have contributed to getting you where you are today. You may recall the desired state for most people is one of safety and security prompted by emotional responses. Unfortunately, the continued response to

emotions leads one to feel out of control, therefore lacking confidence and instilling a feeling of unworthiness."

"The key to tapping back into the mysterious trait known as a humorous disposition is to take risk and accept challenges that will allow your innate sense of spontaneity and curiosity to reignite. The risk can be in any aspect of life. Some people prefer to start off small by taking a different route to work, stopping at a coffee shop you have never supported, ask a colleague whom you have worked with for years to lunch. The risk activity doesn't have to be dramatic; it simply must be an activity that you have consciously selected. This conscious selection (sharp mental focus) contributes to experiencing the sense of control that serves as the foundation for self-confidence. As confidence grows, one feels competent and worthy to pursue greater challenges. This self-altering sequence continues throughout every aspect of one's life, ranging from what you read, where you go, what you wear, to what you eat, and with whom you associate. Some of the most significant gains in self-confidence will emerge as a result of altering entrenched habits and daily routines, and particularly impactful when applied toward free or leisure time."

The simplicity of this technique is a major hurdle for most people, primarily to those existing lower on the emotional tone scale. Their primary response is frequently, "It can't be that easy!" There is a confluence of negative thinking and experience that supports this line of reasoning, so allow me to identify a few of the more entrenched influences. It may have started early in the developmental years with numerous statements and behaviors articulated within the home contributing to a defeatist nature and perhaps reinforced by a peer group of a similar bent. This is the home environment that early on introduces the expectation of danger, pain, disaster, or the like: terror, dread, and apprehension.

There is a time to be afraid, just as there is a time to rejoice; however, for the individual who exists in this chronic fear tone, his solution to life is to be careful. The thought of change creates great anxiety. Psychologically speaking, the difference between fear and anxiety is that in fear the source of the threat is known, whereas in anxiety it is not.

The late Nathaniel Branden conveys the following insights in his book, *Taking Responsibility:* The more we are aware that we choose our actions, the more likely we are to take responsibility for them. Taking responsibility for our actions is a precondition of taking responsibility for our life. Many adults long to remain children and in fact have never ceased being children. They look to others to tell them what to do. One characteristic of successfully evolved adults is that they learn to take responsibility for their own lives physically, emotionally, intellectually, and spiritually.

The predictable response from one who exists in a fear tone is, "It can't be that easy." Underlying this response is the fear that if they were to try to exercise the discipline necessary to alter behavior, the new solution may not work; then where would they be? Hopefully, they will be able to convince all within earshot, "It can't be that easy," therefore avoiding the need to change or, for that matter, even try.

Individuals of a lower level tone will have no trouble finding excuses or justifications why the critical behavior exercise will not work for them; the real concern is how many others will they convince to remain immobile? Even if people are honest with themselves in admitting or recognizing that their critical behaviors are negative, there will be a lifetime of experience to justify a continuation of the negative behavior. One of the best explanations of the phenomena to continue the negative behavior was offered by Dr. Wayne Dyer in his book, *Your Erroneous Zones.* Dyer exposes the four favorite Neurotic Justifications of the American people: *"That's me," "I can't help it," "I've always been that way,"* and *"It's just my nature."* American people believe just by reciting any one of those phrases (listen closely, at times people will insert all four in one sentence), it rids them of any and all accountability and responsibility to change. Please note, Dyer does label them "neurotic" justifications.

The greater the risk or challenge to the individual, the greater the boost to one's self-esteem. I now refer to this as the "Boyle Effect," named after the unemployed and matronly contestant appearing on the 2009 Britain's *Got Talent* show. She stole the hearts of literally millions of viewers around the world when she sang "I Dreamed a Dream" from the play, *Les Miserables.* This moment captured on tape and played over 300,000,000 times on You Tube is one of the most viewed and certainly one of the more moving events recorded in television history.

The judging panel openly admitted to Boyle, *"When you came out, everyone was laughing at you."* Slight pause, *"No one's laughing at you now."* The candor and innocence of her response, *"I've never been given the chance before,"* to the panelist pre-performance questioning as to why she has yet to achieve the celebrity artist recognition for which she aspires, is an inspiration to the world. It is one of the most humbling statements I can recall and yet serves to be one of the most motivational I have heard. I am struck by the reality of the number of people who go unrecognized and unnoticed due to "never having the chance." I am also cognizant of the number of opportunities that exist on a daily basis. The difference is Susan Boyle took a risk while millions of others chose to remain safe.

Similar positive reactions have been recorded by viewers of the popular *Dancing With the Stars* television show with respect to the visible change in self-esteem as celebrities in their own right expand in an arena totally foreign to most: ballroom dancing. In their recorded praise of the show, the participants are quick to verbalize how rewarding it is to be challenged in a skill area in which they had not previously been exposed. All-Pro football players subjecting themselves to the ridicule of mass audiences viewing their attempt to perform a rumba or samba have served as an inspiration for literally millions. This is a sample of the *"Flow"* dynamic that was introduced before, stretching an individual in both skill-related abilities and challenge. And more importantly, they are leaving themselves vulnerable to the criticism of others. This is when true growth takes place. The safety net has been removed.

SECTION 11

THE JOY OF INDEPENDENT THOUGHT AND CHOICE

"*So Dr. Haviland, what would you suggest I should do in order to experience this awakening?*" Rick Myers asked.

"*I wouldn't make a specific suggestion for what another person might do, for the simple reason what might be perceived as a risk by one individual may not be perceived as a risk by another,*" I responded. "*That's why when you witness someone doing something that you and most people consider risky, you can't automatically give them the benefit and label them as high-tone, self-confident, experiencing 'Flow,' or possessing a humorous disposition. They may not view an activity as being risky because they have developed a skill set which minimizes or eliminates the risk in their view. People who participate in sky-diving and mountain climbing really do not have a death wish, contrary to popular belief. They think that people who drive in rush hour traffic and give public speeches do.*"

I can remember when I gave this presentation to a group of physicians at the home of one of the doctors. He was very skeptical of the theory that risk alone could stimulate one's self-confidence and in turn serve to awaken one's humorous disposition that lies dormant.

The host was very insistent that I provide the risk situation for him so that he could experience this growth in self-esteem. The conversation went as follows:

He began, *"So what would you have me do so that I could have this experience?"*

The home audience was very attentive awaiting my response. I gave my explanation about how it was inappropriate for one person to suggest what might be an appropriate risk for another, but he didn't want to hear that, and became more persistent.

"Go ahead. Give me something. Tell me what to do that will tap into this mysterious trait," he insisted.

Given the talk that evening had been well received by those in attendance, I reluctantly made a suggestion in anticipation of moving the program along, *"Okay, Dave, go in the bathroom and shave off your moustache.."*

"What? You mean to tell me, if I go in and shave my moustache it will enhance my sense of humor?" He became fully animated as he was dismissing my suggestion.

"That's about the size of it," I insisted.

"Let me be sure I understand this," he continued. *"If I go in that bathroom and shave my moustache, this will in turn affect my self-confidence certainly related to my personality, thus benefitting my patients in a positive manner?"*

"Spoken like a true physician," I said. At this point, physician Dave was grinning from ear to ear, pacing the floor, trying to contain his laughter, fully animated and spirited. I feel safe in saying few of his colleagues in the room had never seen Dave so alive. He was known around the hospital as being rather stoic and restrained. I didn't have to say another word; those present that evening were seeing a transformation that continued to be the talk of the hospital for weeks to come.

Now to the pertinent question, did he shave it?

Not a chance, as I suspected he wouldn't. So much of one's self-image is influenced by our outward appearance and acceptance by others. The mere suggestion of spontaneously changing one's appearance is sufficient to induce a catatonic state for many, including physicians.

This is why so many of us continue to wear the same hair styles for decades, drive the same make of car, listen to the same music, continue with the same habits, and the list goes on.

I conveyed the moustache story to the class which generated an energetic exchange led by Rick Myers. *"If that doctor had gone in and shaved his moustache, due to the risk involved, he would have contributed to enhancing his sense of humor, or more technically, his humorous disposition. Is that correct?*

"*Spot on,*" I responded and continued. "*What was being demonstrated and obvious to his audience at his house was that the mere thought of shaving the moustache was tapping into something at a psychological level that was totally invigorating. He was experiencing this spontaneous event at the unconscious level, but the animation in his voice and body were manifested for all to see.*"

"*What if he had done it?* Mary Ann asked.

"*I'm not sure what I would have done, other than to point out that the action was commendable and consistent with accepting the challenge, thus contributing to his self-confidence in the long run. My experience and confidence in the theories that we have discussed to date in class made me feel I was on pretty safe ground by making the suggestion at his insistence. He wouldn't do it!*"

"*The risk I took by making the suggestion to the physician was contrary to what I had advised you of before, and that is not to challenge another person because you don't know what they consider risky; therefore, by accepting the challenge, the reality is it may not be risky to them at all. For example, to ask someone to hold a snake would be enough to freak most people out, but to one who was raised near a swampy environment, this may not be a challenging task at all and therefore would have minimal if any impact on their self-esteem. On the other hand, how would they do if asked to give a three minute impromptu speech in front of a class?*"

"*Don't give my doctor friend undue credit. His profession may influence you to perhaps think that he operates at a different level than others because of what he has accomplished. The truth is the doctor has the same insecurities as the rest of us and operates as the rest of us, and those little black hairs above his lip are as precious to him and his perception of himself. It is very unlikely that he would alter that perception in front of* his peers in order to make a point. In some respects, he exists under greater pressure than many community members because he has established himself as a competent individual within the community; therefore, any breach of this may be more detrimental to him. Examples of this extreme pressure are evident when high profile politicians and celebrities, whom society has placed on a pedestal, literally get caught with their pants down. When high profile individuals demonstrate negative CB's, it is difficult for most to comprehend. We expect this behavior from individuals of a lower tone but not from those whom we have elevated in status."

"But Dr. Haviland, don't you think that most people are fearful of this societal judgment coming down on them?" Robin asked.

"Absolutely," was my response. "And that is precisely why we look to others to tell us what is best for us. Think about it. We select a peer group that is accepting of us; we date people who are acceptable to that peer group; we marry people whom our friends approve of; we take jobs that are respectable to others; we live, dress, and drive what is acceptable to others, and we have children and divorce, if approved by others. And I suspect we will ask for advice from others regarding our funerals. No, wait. Insurance companies already tell us what's best for us. So who are we really other than the reflection of whom others want us to be?"

"Think about what we are saying. We live are entire lives from cradle to grave doing what others expect from us in order that we may fit it. And the irony of that is, based on our discussions, if we decide to take charge of our lives by exercising a sharp mental focus, make intelligent decisions instead of emotional ones, and begin to rely on our own judgments rather than the judgments of others…there is a rich, exciting experience that awaits each and every one of us."

"Dr. Haviland, it seems like once it gets rolling on a positive note, everything falls into place.

"Thank you, Mark, but don't be deceived. For everyone who makes it to the sidewalk hall of fame, there is another one who ends up with a tragic story to tell. That's why biographies are so interesting. If you know what you're looking for, it is almost inevitable that you will narrow it down to one individual or one instance when a person allows for mental drift, makes emotional decisions or trusts the judgment of a key person over their own judgment, and the cards begin to fall. This is especially true in the

United States, a society where money, greed, and celebrity are valued so highly by so many. And at the same time, there are so many opportunities to drift and make emotionally bad decisions influenced by individuals who don't necessarily have your best interest at heart.

SECTION 12

THE INFLUENCE OF TECHNOLOGY

In recent history, another way of stating, in my lifetime, it was possible to make a mistake in one of the areas mentioned in the preceding pages, but it wasn't necessarily life altering or damaging. In today's technological society, with our handheld ability to capture every conceivable misdeed for perpetuity, it behooves one not to make a mistake. In days of yesteryear, improprieties were very hush-hush and kept within the family. Today, one is fortunate if they can make it to the comfort of their home before the misdeed becomes fodder for anyone who has access to electronic or mobile communication devices. The potential for outside persecution is immediate, unforgiving, and lifelong. Rarely does a week go by when we don't read about an individual taking one's life due to the anticipation of the consequences any one inappropriate action may bring upon that person.

What are the implications of this dynamic as it relates to one's emotional tone or self-esteem? We can already see the influence, as subtle as it may be. We are a society becoming increasingly aware of the exposure and possible ridicule we may receive as a result of any one action that we may commit or opinion we express; therefore, we are withdrawing. We are reluctant to get involved or voice an opinion. Let me clarify that. We are reluctant to get involved when we risk the chance of being identified as a participant. The irony is we frequently want to express an opinion provided we remain anonymous, and many thought that access to the Internet would provide that sanctuary or refuge. Unfortunately, many have learned the hard way that the anticipated anonymity of the Internet is more fantasy than reality.

Recognizing the vulnerability and exposure that comes with involvement, we are increasingly becoming a nation of spectators opposed to a nation of participants. One fourth of prime time television viewing is now comprised of "reality programming." Reality programs could be called "living your life vicariously." How much this transition from being one actively involved in life to one willing to view it only from a distance may be attributed to one's fear of exposure or criticism cannot be determined. The transition has been sluggish in nature but very apparent with each generation.

Within my lifetime, I have witnessed school kids race from school to get on their bikes and pedal to the nearest ball field or engage in make-believe war games as they raced through the woods. Students now wait to be picked up from school, may have a snack when they get home, and then retreat to their room. They emerge from their rooms for dinner that is frequently devoured in front of the television or in competition with social media.

This observation is not to be critical, merely to point out that somewhere along this journey through life, the conclusion was made that it is safer or more rewarding to experience the path traveled by others than to brave our own way. I laughed the first time I saw bowling on television, and I recall making the statement, "Who in the world would sit and watch someone else bowl?" Well, I've learned to keep my mouth shut as I've watch a variety of events generate tremendous viewer support as we tune in to watch others play pool and even cards.

What does it say about our society when *Fifty Shades of Gray* is a bestseller and a record breaking movie at the box office starring two unknown actors? There was a time when the mere suggestion that one would give up participation in a pleasurable activity in order to watch another participate in the same activity was inconceivable.

The introduction of the above topic in the classroom set off a lively debate as a variety of television programming equally divided those who supported a specific program versus critics who couldn't conceive of anyone vicariously enjoying watching someone else play golf, cook, drive a car around a circular track, arrange flowers, or run around an island naked.

"So what's so bad about living this vicarious experience?" Kim inquired.

I offered the following explanation, "*It isn't a question of good or bad. It's the reality that by willingly giving up the experience of participation (living), one is yielding part of oneself to the control of others. In essence, it's the difference between living and taking up space. This lies at the very heart or crossroads of the curiosity and spontaneity of the child yearning to participate by yelling out, 'Pick me, pick me.' How often have you heard a child yell out, 'Don't pick me. I'd rather watch'?*"

Something is happening in our society that is making it more comfortable to participate electronically and anonymously from the comfort of the coffeehouse, camouflaged in passwords and passcodes, than in person. At the same time, there is awareness that the security that has been assumed to be impenetrable is also a myth. While these two remain in conflict, our ability to communicate from one individual to another has been compromised.

"*Wow. I think I'm finally catching on,*" Chrystal Shannon offered. "*It is virtually impossible to choose to be a spectator in life seeking safety and security, avoiding risk and challenge, and at the same time having high self-esteem.*"

"*Why would anyone choose not to have high self-esteem?*" was Robin's question.

Carol responded. "*Can I answer?*"

"*Go for it,*" I urged.

"*It's not really a conscious choice. In some respects, early on we have limited control because we are the product of the influences of our home environment and parental influence. The socialization process begins, and we yield to the peer group that is most receptive to us with all the emotional highs and lows that accompany that developmental process,*" she concluded.

"So it's not my fault I'm so screwed up?" Sam inserted.

My response, *"There is some truth to that. Unfortunately, there does come a point when you must assume responsibility for your actions and become aware that behaviors have consequences. And this is where it gets a bit more complicated because there is no set time or age when this crossroad occurs."*

"If you had to guess, when would you say it occurs?" Reid asked.

"Again, impossible to pin it down due to the diverse backgrounds we represent; however, we certainly can identify some stages that one would suspect would be critical in forcing these choices that are so instrumental in our development," I offered.

"Like when?" Jason prompted.

I responded, *"In addition to the home environment experienced in our youth, I would suggest the selection and activities of a specific peer group would be huge in influencing one's ultimate disposition. In the old days it was the smokers versus the non-smokers, the jocks versus the hoods, the band members versus the drama club, and the list goes on. The point being, during those formative years, it is difficult for one to be proactive and maintain a sharp mental focus. The truth of the matter is we are adrift, and the primary influence on which way we go is frequently determined by which group is the most accepting of us."*

Parental influence also becomes a major player during these formative years. This is obvious with examples like regulating study time and curfews, especially once driving privileges are granted. Bear in mind, some individuals never do assume responsibility for their actions, and I think we have all witnessed this. It is easy to envision for many students who attend college apart from what they do with their free time, true independence and decision making may be postponed until graduation."

"But eventually we are faced with the big three CB's, is that correct?" Marti quizzed.

"Precisely," I concurred.

"Would you say one's 'emotional tone' is established before or after the CB's come into play?" Jennifer asked.

"I think it's safe to say the emotional tone is established rather early, primarily due to the parental influence in the home environment. We pick

up their cues as to whether or not this world is a safe, adventurous place to live or if every situation holds an element of danger. However, as much as we would like to lay the blame at the feet of our parents, we eventually are responsible for the decisions we make, which in turn influence our movement on the tone scale," I summarized.

"The good news is, regardless of the past influences, we modify and mold what currently is by the decisions we make in the next year, month, week, day, and hour. We become the architects of our future; that's why I like that CB exercise. We identify what behaviors are taking us where we want to go and continue to reinforce them while eliminating those actions which are counterproductive to where we want to go and who we want to be." I was enthused.

Glenn Wright contributed, "And if I understand this in its entirety, it is essential that one have high self-esteem and exist high on the emotional tone scale in order to experience 'Flow' and possess the humorous disposition essential to lead."

"Accurate, to the letter," I responded. "Class dismissed."

PART III

DIFFUSING CONFLICT

SECTION 13

THE ABILITY TO DIFFUSE CONFLICT

Energized by my students', I began my quest in earnest. What is it that makes an individual virtually "priceless" to some organizations? My focus would not be centered on the individual whose contribution was obvious, usually due to their creative genius, ala Steven Jobs. I would focus on the individual who is characterized as the indispensable leader, and those qualities that make them indispensable, or for the purpose of this study, priceless.

Completing an exhaustive search of contemporary literature addressing "leadership," it was generally agreed that most effective leaders possessed specific traits, or a combination and blending of traits. The following is a listing of traits, most frequently attributed to leaders:

a) Charismatic
b) Self-confident
c) Visionary
d) Self-motivated
e) Creative

f) Trusting
g) Communicative
h) Intelligent
i) Humorous
j) Energetic
k) Optimistic

Admittedly, it was relatively easy to identify the "leadership" traits, or blending thereof, in most individuals recognized as leaders in contemporary society, or "leaders" from a historical perspective. In some cases, biographers' have not been exceptionally generous in their endorsement of a specific trait, however even the critics were reluctant to cite glaring omissions of the above traits in recognized leaders. Even the "Scourge of God," Attila the Hum appears to be a liberal blend of the above traits, according to historians.

In our highly technological society, able to electronically retrieve the most minute transgression, it will be increasingly difficult for one to be recognized as a "leader." Leaders of today are under attack. Much of that attack stems from our disappointment when individuals fail to meet the demanding expectations we place on them.

Given the potential for so many people to have all, if not most, or at least a blending of the above traits; Why is there such an absence of leadership in this country today? Why is it when we exercise our civic duty and vote, a great percentage of the candidates run unopposed? Certainly, the characteristics are not so complex, or so rare, to preclude a full slate of candidates.

Some would suggest, the absence of leaders and leadership is easily understood given the insecurity of the present. Warren Bennis offers some insights from his perspective of one placed in a leadership position. As a distinguished professor of business administration at the University of Southern California Bennis offers a unique insight in his work; Why Leaders Can't Lead: The Unconscious Conspiracy. The revelation came to Bennis while President of the University of Cincinnati, and failing to make the progress he had anticipated. In a moment of discovery, he states: "I had become the victim of a vast, amorphous, unwitting, unconscious conspiracy to prevent me from doing anything whatever to change the university's status quo." A discovery experienced by many who have been elevated or appointed to positions of leadership, regardless of the industry or institution, profit or non-profit, service or manufacturing. The dynamics are the same, a conspiracy to smother all creative planning, and all fundamental change in the institution.

One could certainly argue that these times of unprecedented technological influence, expanding markets, and domestic instability will serve to solidify the conspiracy to an even greater extent than currently exist. The above two phenomenon, may appear contradictory at first blush. On the one hand, the suggestion is that the conspiracy is stifling change, and on the other hand, the suggestion is the rate of change is unprecedented. The two are not mutually exclusive. The irony is that the change which is taking place is not being orchestrated by "leaders," but by individuals and organizations who are forced into "leadership roles," then exposed to the inevitable conspiracy that seeks to bog and preserve the present.

Look for progress to be made by the persevering entrepreneur who holds tenaciously to dreams of yesteryear and ignores the bureaucracy that seeks to impede. Computer conglomerates will be nurturing quality circles, and employee stock option plans long into the night, while Bill Gates continues to move technology forward. Proprietary schools of technology will emerge, while established institutions continue to bicker over equitable work loads and parking lot preference.

An insightful definition of leadership, amidst the 600 odd offerings is: Leadership; is the ability to be out of control-comfortably. Individuals in contemporary leadership positions will survive in their current positions, if they are willing to accept and work within the confines of a conspiracy which gives lip service, but covertly loathes change.

Another well camouflaged nemesis on the landscape is the individual who subjects oneself to a leadership position, in order to lead the flock. Predictably, wherever the flock ends, will no doubt be advantages to the security of the "leader."

Acknowledging the limitations of pursuing evidence of the cited "traits" of a leader by virtue of position, I began to cross reference "leaders" with evidence of the specific traits listed. A similar approach to John Naisbitts' "content analysis" employed in his best seller "Megatrends." My goal; to note, if and when, the identifiable traits previously listed are evident in individuals who are traditionally recognized as "leaders." If evidence of the trait exists, is there an additional correlation to be found in reference to earning power? The degree to which a trait exists is subjective, nevertheless, somewhat universal in acceptance.

For the most part, in recognized leaders, there is little difficulty finding supportive evidence for the existence of the majority of the identifiable leadership traits listed at the beginning of the chapter. However, the specific trait of humor, is far more challenging to document due to the difficulty in defining what it is, and if in fact it is present. Humor began to take on the dynamics of beauty, i.e. difficult to define, but we know it when we see it.

I was surprised to find the indispensable quality was not very well hidden, and not, I might add, a quality that was reserved for a select few. It was a quality inherent in all, however refined by only a select few.

The research focused on individuals who are, or were, placed in leadership positions in order to reduce the criticism relating to whether or not they were "leaders." This determination holds all the potential to totally bog any progress that may be made, and take on the feared characteristics of the "conspiracy" alluded to previously. For the skeptic among us, there is no pretense that this is a scientific study subject to control groups and other impediments reserved for the sacred halls. It is merely an observational study, with the expectation that the results may assist those souls who seek enlightenment as to why certain individuals succeed and subsequently earn considerably more than others.

It seems appropriate to begin with a case study of an individual who in response to the Knight-Ridder Newspaper survey question, "If you were given the opportunity to spend an evening with any one person, living, deceased or fictional, whom would you choose and why?" Finishing third behind God and Jesus; Lee Iacocca, an individual who certainly manifests many of the leadership traits previously listed.

Lido Anthony Iacocca, the blunt-talking, cigar-chomping, former truck salesman is the "best corporate motivator of this century" according to automobile industry analyst for Keane Securities in

Detroit. He has risen to the status of folk hero as a result of the Iacocca touch, the touch that gave us the Ford Mustang, the Mercury Cougar, the Chrysler K-cars, the minivan and the Jeep. He is one of the few individuals alive, who is taken seriously, when offering to take over the Chrysler Corporation.

Author, and biographer Peter Wyden reserves the following for Iacocca. "Brilliant. Tough. Charismatic. A national hero with phenomenal name recognition. Superb communicator. Virtous negotiator and administrator. His curiosity and appetite for new ways to solve problems suggest a capacity to adapt to new crises."

Iacocca confronted the "conspiracy" that would seek to undermine his leadership directly, "We're having more success with our union. They see the handwriting on the wall. They have got to work on quality just as we do. Is this the honeymoon or will we get back to adversarial approaches again?" Iacocca transformed a company from bankruptcy to success, paying off a controversial $1.2 billion bail-out government loan seven years early.

What's it worth to an organization to have an individual with this degree of influence? In Iacocca's case, we all know, as a result of the widely publicized announcement by the Chrysler Corp. that he would receive $17.9 million for the year. So that the layman among us can relate, that converts to an hourly salary of $8,653.85. Now we can all relate! Admittedly the bulk of that monstrous sum was from stock appreciation. When Iacocca was confronted about the announcement of his princely award at a news conference, his response was met with loud applause, and an echo of adulation from all present. "I was embarrassed," he said. "But what should I do? Should I root for the stock to go down?"

Was Iacocca really that valuable to the Chrysler Corp.? Or is it the perception of the American public, and ultimately the stockholders, that create the value? I suspect there are countless engineers employed by Chrysler who know considerably more about the mechanics and technology in the latest model year than Lee Iacocca.

How would the contemporary director of human resources treat Iacocca's application if it came across their desk:

White male, mid-60's, recently divorced from second wife and estranged from his third, fired after 32 years at Ford Motor Co., and recently accused of possibly staying too long at Chrysler. Enjoys community service work although was asked to leave extremely visible campaign chairmanship. Is considered to be inflexible and egotistical, however willing to consider and negotiate any offer in the $8,000 per hour range.

Just makes one want to reach for the telephone doesn't it? Perhaps his public response to the above concerns shed some light on his true value to an organization. His light hearted dismissal to the outrageous salary has been noted. In response to his dismissals from Ford and the reconstruction of Ellis Island he responded; "I've got to stop getting fired like this."

He openly admits to the loneliness he experienced after his wife Mary's untimely death as a result of diabetes, and his own fear of dying alone. He candidly admits he probably should have waited a little longer before marrying Peggy Johnson, which was dissolved after 19 months. He admits that he wasn't sure in his heart if he was done mourning his first wife.

His glaring openness is in stark contrast to his ability to easily afford isolation, and be non-committal to any personal issues. He chooses to be open and able to diffuse personal attacks. In response to the badgering that takes place each election year regarding his presidential aspirations he quips; "That he has no political ambitions, and would appreciate a different line of questioning." He adds further clarification, "I find that line of questioning tiresome, and besides it makes my campaign manager nervous!" The room erupts in laughter.

With Iacocca's ability to relate and communicate, it comes as no surprise that his autobiography, Iacocca, became the best-selling hardcover autobiography in history (2.6 million copies). Who does a man like Iacocca, with what appears to be an unlimited supply of admirers look up to? He reserves a special place for an individual who took the time to call and provide comfort and assurance during Lee's time of need when his wife, Mary, was in intensive care in a coma. The caller Ronald Reagan, President of the United States.

Iacocca states, "You know, in life there are some people you meet whom you'd just like to pal around with. They're fun, they put you in a good frame of mind, and they make you feel terrific. Well that's Ronald Reagan." An early memory Iacocca has of Reagan was a Sunday evening dinner at the White House. The evening conversation would focus on free trade and economic affairs, consistent with the expertise in the room. "After the dinner Reagan had dismissed all the help. The President himself was walking around the table pouring us French wine. I can still hear him whispering to me as he was filling my glass: "Don't tell anybody, but I found a couple of good French bottles lying around. My friends from California would probably go nuts if they knew I served French wine to you guys." Iacocca adds; "There's no way on earth you could dislike him."

Lee Iacocca was not alone in his praise of Ronald Reagan, and certainly historians will have a field day with his contribution to this nation. In many ways the man remains an enigma. The Los Angeles Times Syndicate reports that Ronald Reagan ended his term of office with the highest approval rating of any president since Franklin Roosevelt. As recently as January '95, Reagan ranks third behind Dwight Eisenhower and Rev. Billy Graham in a USA Today poll of "Men We Admire."

A Star Tribune article attributes the political rout of 1984 to the Democrats picking the wrong enemy-Ronald Reagan. "The Democrats wanted to make the elections a referendum not on president Clinton's two years in office, but rather on former President Reagan's tenure. Consistent with this approach, the Democrats announced a theme for the elections 'Don't go back'-and claimed constantly that Republican candidates wanted to return to 'the failed policies of the past.'"

"The Democrats' strategy was, we now know, a miserable failure. To the extent that voters accepted the Democrats' invitation to treat the election as a test of Clintonomics vs. Reaganomics, Reaganomics won hands down."

A majority now feel that Reagan will go down in history as an "outstanding" or "above average" president. What makes this assessment more startling is that majorities in the Media General Associated Press survey gave negative grades to Reagan's social policies and ethics enforcement, rated his judgement unfavorably and said they would not have supported him for a third term.

Reagan received negative ratings for his handling of every social issue posed: civil rights, 51 percent negative; education, 54 percent negative; housing, 65 percent negative, and welfare, 67 percent negative. Six in 10 rated him negatively on his handling of ethics in government. On the other hand the same survey noted two-thirds rated his leadership ability as excellent or good. A full three-quarters favorably rated his charisma and ability to communicate. What's with this guy?

Reagan's historical defeat of Walter Mondale (523-13 Electoral College votes) in 1984 is significant in that Walter Mondale had the endorsement of the national teachers union, the major labor organization and the National Organization for Women, in addition to his historic nomination of Geraldine Ferraro to share the Democratic ticket. Mondale had defeated the "Great Communicator" in the first nationally televised debate, however an incident in the second debate may be a critical insight exemplifying Reagan's power to communicate so effectively. When the issue of Reagan's advancing age came up, as we all knew it would, he responded; "I will not make age an issue in this campaign. I am not going to exploit, for political purposes, my opponent's youth and inexperience." At that precise moment, the election was over. Our fearless leader had been on the ropes, but in the end he had delivered the knockout punch.

This knockout punch delivered by Reagan brought to mind a knockout punch that had earlier been delivered by Mondale. Gary Hart received the knockout blow at that time. Mondale and Hart were in a virtual deadlock for the Democratic presidential nomination in 1984, when they engaged in a nationally televised debate. In the most eloquent fashion Hart waxed on about the social programs his administration would introduce. There he sat, extremely confident, handsome, and articulate holding the audience spellbound in anticipation of what could be. The significance of the soliloquy dismissed in a moment by Mondale, as he offered his rebuttal in a quip from a popular Wendy's hamburger commercial, "Where's the beef?" The response captured the cover story of the next issue of Newsweek magazine. Again, the knockout blow had been delivered.

More recently, Ross Perot dismissed an assault on the inappropriateness of his candidacy due to his lack of political experience, by offering; "You're right, I don't know what it is to run up a four trillion-dollar debt." Ironically, after the audience laughter abated, the issue was never revisited.

Are these knockout punches unrehearsed, and totally spontaneous, as they appear to be? Roger Ailes advisor and coach to Ronald Reagan for the president's crucial second debate with Walter Mondale, would have us believe otherwise in his book; You Are the Message-Secrets of the Master Communicators. Ailes suggest that TV has changed the way we view the world. As a result of TV, people today expect to be made comfortable in every communications situation. We are unconsciously judged by our audience against the standards set by TV personalities. "You're expected to be at least as comfortable, knowledgeable, and to the point as any good guest on a television show. Subconsciously, the style that's acceptable on television-relaxed, informal crisp, and entertaining-becomes the modern standard for an effective communicator." "Ronald Reagan's greatest gift is not his speaking ability but his ability to make others comfortable."

In "The Acting President," author Gary Paul Gates reflects, "I think the general attitude of the public was that Reagan was like a loveable uncle." To some extent, says Gates, "The media was caught up in the illusions. Ronald Reagan was a enormously likeable guy, and I think the press liked the anecdotes (and) they liked the one liners, too." Most readers are familiar with Reagan's one liners that captured national attention, namely immediately following the assassination attempt on his life when he confronted his wife outside the emergency room and quipped: "Honey, I forgot to duck." In viewing the team of surgeons about to remove the bullet lodged in his chest he quips "I hope you're all Republicans."

The bottom line is, the ability to defuse a tense situation with the use of humor creates an overall perception of self-confidence. The public identifies with the individuals' self-confidence and transfers the same unto themselves, both individually and collectively. Therefore, in Reagan the American public was given back her self-confidence, her self-respect and her status as a world leader. Ronald Reagan took a nation that was meandering spiritually and gave it a sense of purpose, a renewed vigor and feelings of hope."

Reagan was the first president since another Republican-Dwight Eisenhower, who held office from 1953 to 1961to serve two full terms and the first president in 60 years to turn the White House over to a successor of his own party.

The message was not lost on George Bush, Reagan's successor. Bush was quick to point out that his opponent Michael Dukakis' foreign affairs experience amounts to "eating breakfast once at the International House of Pancakes." Another in the same vein goes, "Dukakis thinks a foreign market is a place where you go to buy French bread." Make no mistake, there is no intent here to suggest that George Bush shared the same magic as the charismatic Ronald Reagan. What he did share was the knowledge that a poignant comment made at a critical time, does wonders in influencing the perception of the public. This knowledge was strongly influenced during his forceful exchange with newscaster Dan Rather. In one verbal exchange, Bush was transformed from wimp to buff stud, in the eyes of the public. Incidentally, in a political race, those are the only eyes that count.

Another contemporary Republican family that was well schooled by Reagan was the Dole family. Certainly, the jury is still out regarding the mark to be left by Senator Robert Dole and his wife Elizabeth, on the political front. However, his wife Elizabeth is an interesting study pertaining to effective communicators. Elizabeth Dole was Secretary of Transportation under President Reagan and Secretary of Labor under Bush. Her public service record is long and distinguished. She has served under every president from Lyndon B. Johnson to George Bush and recently gave up her governmental hat to take on the leadership of the American Red Cross. I personally championed her to be the first woman in the White House.

The endorsement of Elizabeth Dole as the first female president is not predicated on her vast experience, but more importantly on her ability to communicate effectively with the public. Her husband's political career may have been saved due to her ability to recover for him. When Robert Dole won the Iowa primary and appeared to be the Republican to beat, he was asked by a reporter, what the significance of his victory might be, and more pointedly how his election to the White House might affect his wife Elizabeth. His response is noteworthy: "If elected, I'll be in the white House making decisions, and she'll (Elizabeth) be in the White House making beds." A damning remark in today's gender conscious society. The remark, that may have fallen other political hopefuls without adequate protection, barely saw the light of day in the news media, thanks to Elizabeth's ability to defuse the situation. Her response, to reporters sensing front page material? "In no way do I feel slighted by Bob's remark. We banter back and forth like that all the time. The well informed know that no one is more supportive to my career than Bob, and besides, we know who really makes the bed." The knockout punch that may have saved a political career.

Interestingly, Ronald Reagan appears to be an avid admirer of Abraham Lincoln, and refers to him frequently. It is no wonder that Reagan would be a admirer of Lincoln's, an individual who is recognized for his ability to defuse conflict, with the use of one liners. Volumes have been written about the humor of Lincoln. Perhaps a favorite occurred during one of the Lincoln-Douglas debates when Douglas referred to Lincoln as being wishy-washy, hypocritical, and two-faced. To which Lincoln slowly approached the platform and responded; "I've just been accused of being twofaced. Now I ask you. Do you think if I had two faces, I would choose this one?" The reaction of the crowd was predictable—spontaneous laughter. There is power in communicating effectively!

As historians review the careers of prominent politicians with an influence that lingers to this day, there is a reoccurring trait that is pronounced; their ability to laugh at themselves, and defuse hostility with humor.

Politicians will be quick to point out the tremendous charisma and ability to communicate effectively demonstrated by John F. Kennedy as a case in point. Individuals who study humor will be quick to point out his willingness to make fun of his youth, Catholicism, wealth and inexperience as he pursued the highest office in the land. In 1960, when faced with the challenge presented by Hubert Humphrey, Kennedy responded: "Hubert's problem is that he has too many ideas and too much energy. He alarms the country. I think the people want a less controversial and more boring candidate. Someone like me."

In "All the Presidents' Wits," author Gerald Gardner says "It's a toss-up between Kennedy and Reagan. Both have been very adroit in using humor to ingratiate themselves and to defuse sensitive issues." According to Gardner if Richard Nixon had the same White House wit, he might have been able to weather Watergate. Nixon didn't have the ability to laugh at himself or the world.

Gardner's book examines Reagan and the five preceding administrations. "Ford is able to joke about his own flaws, which is why I think he's so immensely likeable," Gardner said. There was a cutting edge to Jimmy Carter's humor, he said. "He once began a press conference by saying: 'I don't have very much for you gentleman today, so you can put away your crayons."

Lyndon Johnson's humor was earthy, folksy, and sometimes crude, according to Gardner.

Historical accounts of individual contributions made by leaders become distorted by vested interest, and certainly dated attempts at humor lose all significance. However, theologian Eldon Trueblood offers a unique perspective of a leader of 2000 years ago. In his work: The Humor of Christ, Trueblood suggests that Christ' ability to hold the attention of the multitudes, was in part a result of his ability to use humor effectively.

Modern theologians have attempted to translate every word uttered by Christ to be some very esoteric message. In reality, according to Trueblood, when Christ spoke in parables, he was relating to the audience in a manner acceptable, and meaningful at the time. If one is receptive to this theory, the parable of the camel getting through the eye of the needle, as being analogous to the rich man getting into heaven, takes on an entirely new interpretation.

One can only speculate what significance Walter Mondale's quip: "Where's the beef?" will take on when historians decipher the message in the year 4000, two thousand years from now.

In Mark McCormack's; What They Didn't Teach You at Harvard Business School, he cites a sense of humor as the second most important trait necessary for success. The first? Common sense. Let's exam this sixth sense-the sense of humor.

SECTION 14

———◆✕◆———

HUMOR ITS ORIGIN AND POWER

Taken literally, the term humor is borrowed from the Latin, according to Wilfred Funk, the author of Word Origins and Their Romantic Stories. Funk states, "We borrowed the term bodily from the Latin, and in that language humor meant a liquid. Apparently the ancient philosophers believed that four liquids entered into the make-up of our bodies, and that our temperament (Latin temperamentum, mixture) was determined by the proportions of four fluids or humors, which are blood, phlegm, bile, and black bile." If one happened to have an overplus of "blood," the first of the humors, they were of the optimistic and sanguine temperament (Latin sanguis, blood). A generous portion of phlegm, on the other hand, made one "phlegmatic," or slow and unexcitable. Too much yellow bile and one saw the world through a "bilious" eye, and since the word "bile" is chole in Latin, one were apt to be choleric and short-tempered. The fourth humor, and the non-existent black bile, was a little special invention of the ancient physiologists. A too heavy proportion of this made one "melancholy" for in Latin melancholia meant "the state of having too much black bile." Any imbalance of these humors, therefore, made a person unwell and perhaps eccentric. Over the years the word humor took on the meaning of "oddness," and a humorous individual was one who we would now call a crank. Finally, the word was applied to those who could provoke laughter at the oddities and the incongruities of life. Humor is a compassionate account of human beings caught in the drama of living.

Laboring under no delusions of being an etiologist, I would suggest that a common definition of a sense of humor would include not only the individual who has the ability to provoke laughter, but has the ability to appreciate the incongruity which ultimately generates laughter. The close relationship between a healthy person (humorous), and laughter, further explains the inappropriate juxtaposition of humor and comedy.

Acknowledging Funk's contribution in defining humor, I would be remiss if I didn't provide his insight attesting to the origin of the word comedy in order to complete the distinction of the two; humor and comedy.

According to Funk, in the Greece of two millenniums ago, a komos was a festival with music and dancing that lasted until after supper and ended with a torchlight parade. These drunken celebrations were devised by Dorians, a sturdy Hellenic tribe noted for their bawdy humor. The earlier revels were characterized by absolute license, as also were the early comedies. The chief singer at the party was the komoidos, or comedian, and from this Greek term we derive the word comedy.

I'm not sure to whom I am beholden, the Greeks, the Latins, or Funk. In any event, the distinction between humor and comedy becomes clear. This should be comforting to those individuals who do not relish the "lamp shade command performance" usually associated with comedians, and yet covet the rewards associated with a keen sense of humor.

There appears to be a limited relationship between the two words, humor and comedy, when taken literally. When confronted to cite the difference between the two, I usually reference the former Tonight show as an example. Johnny Carson was the obvious "comic", while Ed McMahon may in fact possess the desired "sense of humor."

Psychologist Allen Klein, a nationally known lecturer on health and humor, and the author of The Healing Power of Humor, states; "Humor is more than joke telling. Humor is an attitude, a way of looking at life. It's very powerful because it gives us a different perspective."

There is a warmth and non-judgmental disposition which radiates from an individual with a well developed sense of humor. They are sensitive, receptive, and accepting of others and their ideas. The reasons for this will be discussed at length, later in the chapter. This perceived sensitivity, or sixth sense is what culminates in effective communication and subsequently "worth" to the organization. What is the origin of this "sixth sense?"

It is ironic that we categorize humor along with the other senses; sight, touch, hearing, smell, and taste and yet usually refer to "developing one's sense of humor" while acknowledging the decline of the other senses as we age. How, or does in fact, this sense differ from the others? I surmise, that it doesn't.

One of the most notable authors addressing the origins of humor was the eminent Sigmund Freud. In his work; Jokes and Their Relations to the Unconscious, Freud points out that smiling, a precursor to humor, is evident as early as the first week in a newborn child. The first smiles were experienced during sleep, however, within the month smiles were apparent while fully alert, usually following a feeding, and in response to voice and tactile stimulation.

At two months, a child grins at sights and sounds, and within the first half year of life laughter begins as a result of discriminate recognition, referred to as schema according to Piaget. Following this initial exposure to the world the entire phenomena of the smile, laugh, and development of one's sense of humor become more complex. Paul McGhee's work supports this evolutionary process in his contribution; Humor: Its Origin and Development.

Child psychiatrist John F. Schowalter, M.D., at Yale University's Child Study Center confirms that a sense of humor begins to develop during the very first months of life. Though these little laughs are not something dramatically new to any mother who has chuckled along with her baby, what is new is the curiosity experts have shown in recent years about how children's emotions grow.

It is interesting to note that some researchers believe that this recognition/smile phenomena is what also creates value in works of art. Unknown works of art create limited recognition and response, and consequently have modest value compared to specific works or individual styles that are immediately recognized. Therein lies the "true value" or in many cases the "priceless" value associated with a masterpiece. Therefore, it is not necessarily the beauty, form, or color of a work that creates the value, it may be more importantly, the immediate recognition of the style that creates the value.

I had an opportunity to challenge this theses while visiting the Louvre in Paris. It was the exceptional person (or I might add the very tired person), who did not break out in a wide grin when confronting the works: Mona Lisa, Venus de Milo, and Whistler's Mother. The reception and the response to a recognizable work of art becomes very predictable.

In addition to the enjoyment generated by familiar visual stimulation, the same holds true as a result of auditory stimulation as a result of introducing familiar sounds. Repeating similar verbal sounds, which occur in verse, make use of the same source of pleasure-the rediscovery of something familiar. In this context there is a suggestion that a close connection exists between recognition, remembering, and enjoyment. Certainly, the proliferation of "oldies but goodies" radio stations would support this thesis.

Freud also alludes to the importance of recognition in his work; Jokes and Their relationship to the Unconscious. He states; "Recognition is always, unless too mechanized, linked with feelings of pleasure." An example of this is when a speaker asks the question, How many of you have ever . . . ? Usually, the question is one in which the answer is predictably affirmative, i.e. How many of you have ever felt rushed during the holiday season? Nevertheless, our participation, by raising our hand in the affirming manner, is frequently accompanied with approving nods and verbal affirmation, serving to unite the audience. In any event, a pleasurable mutual experience, accentuates the commonality of the group, which heretofore was not evident.

The act of recognition gives rise to pleasure. This basis of joy in recognition, is the bases of the enjoyment of art. Recognition also plays a major role in the appreciation of jokes which is so frequently associated with comedy and humor. The ability to appreciate jokes is the ability to find similarity between dissimilar things-that is, hidden similarities. The broader one's perspective, and the more vast one's experiences, the greater one's reservoir of dissimilar things to draw from. Hence the suggestion that one's intellectual capacity or experiential learning may be a precursor to their enjoyment of life and ultimately to the development of one's sense of humor. Laughter binds people together through the sense of a "shared experience" even with a stranger. This cohesiveness decreases stress and hence illness, probably because of the belief that we are not alone with our troubles.

On the other hand, a limited background of experiences and exposure to diverse cultures, etc. may explain why humor of a more base or ribald nature may be enjoyed by a particular segment of the population. This segment of the population may not have had the opportunities, or were denied exposure, opposed to another more diverse segment of the population.

Topicality, especially timely topicality is based on the pleasure derived from new interest of the day, i.e. jokes have a limited life span. Witticism that is familiar and fresh yields pleasure and is rewarded by applause. This realization may play a part in solving the riddle of why many older people appear to have lost their sense of humor as they age. Elderly people may not stay abreast of recent events; therefore, few things appear familiar. This further explains the apparent endless popularity of comics from the George Burns, Bob Hope era. Appreciation of their contributions (oneliners), does not hinge on the knowledge of the events of the previous twenty-four hours, as required of a David Letterman or Jay Leno audience.

The question now becomes; What value can be placed on an individual who can generate the same sort of receptiveness from an employee within an organization, as the masterpiece does from the spectator at the museum? Is $18 million dollars a year a reasonable figure? Or better yet, how often do you think Lee Iacocca has to introduce himself?

Contemplate for a moment the worth of a CEO, supervisor, or line worker whose disposition is as predictable as is the recognition of a master work of art. Furthermore, assume they possess the "Sixth sense", that of a sense of humor, with all the attributes we had previously assigned, namely a receptiveness to others and their ideas. What's their worth to the organization?

Humor can be a potent tool in the office or the factory to ease tension, improve morale, and increase efficiency, claims Peter Desberg, a professor of graduate education studies at California State University, and the author of six books on humor. "Humor doesn't function as a panacea. But a person who can use humor successfully has a definite advantage." Humor can be a means of reinterpreting situations that will keep you from becoming too angry, anxious, or depressed. "Look at something a different way to see the absurdity of the situation."

The Futurist magazine reports a study at Black Hawk College in Moline, Illinois, which found a close relationship between the willingness to laugh in all kinds of situations and the capacity to form successful relationships, both in the family and in the business and professional world.

According to Dr. William F. Fry, a psychiatrist affiliated with Stanford University who has been a student of laughter for three decades; "Laughter stimulates the production of alertness hormones called catecholamine. These hormones in turn trigger the release of endorphins in the brain. Endorphins, which have been likened to nature's Valium, foster a sense of relaxation and well-being and dull the perception to pain.

Robert Half International, an executive recruiting firm in New York, conducted a survey of vice presidents and personnel directors at 100 of the USA's largest corporations. Results: 84 percent of the executives said employees with a sense of humor did a better job.

"People with a sense of humor tend to be more creative less rigid and more willing to consider and embrace new ideas and methods," says Half.

The primary evidence when a sense of humor is lacking. In a word 'defensiveness'. The corollaries, appear to be true also. It begs the question to suggest that one lacking a sense of humor (open-mindedness), would be readily open to new ideas, methods and creativity.

The argument would not be; Is it possible for one to be creative, and yet defensive? The timelier argument would be; Is it possible for one who has expressed creativity before, to be receptive to constructive input, and if so, to what degree? I would suggest, regardless of evidence of earlier creativity, the likelihood of one who is presently lacking in humor, to be receptive or open minded, is remote. A defensive attitude would prevail.

Daniel Goleman, in his work; Working with Emotional Intelligence provides some interesting insights in the section entitled, What Employers Want. He indicates employers are complaining; "Too many young people can't take criticism—they get defensive or hostile when people give them feedback on how they're doing. They react to performance feedback as though it was a personal attack."

Creativity is defined as combining known information in unusual ways to make something new that is pleasing, useful, or both. Notice the similarity between our earlier definition of one with a sense of humor as being healthy and open to others and their ideas, and Susan Goodman's insights in her article; Creativity. "Creativity begins with the right attitude: openness, flexibility, a willingness to see new ideas."

According to David Perkins, Harvard Graduate School of Education, "Creative people accept confusion and uncertainty. In fact, they come to view it as normal, even interesting. And they learn that with risk comes reward." Compare Perkins' contribution with my favorite definition of Leadership gleaned from the efforts of the past two decades of research on the subject. "Leadership is the ability to be out of control comfortably." Only in our inappropriate quest to gain control over those individuals and circumstances within our domain do we fail in our desire to lead. Is this the secret to unlimited value to the organization? Or inadvertently, is the key to ineffective leadership, an unyielding attempt to be in control?

I am indebted to Harvey Mindess and his work, Laughter and Liberation; in which he examines the liberating effect of developing one's sense of humor. "Laughter can liberate you from fear, sorrow, tension, and inhibition. It can extricate you from awkward, terrifying, or uncontrollable situations. It can make a humdrum life bearable, and add enjoyment to a coffee break."

In the introductory chapter which states; "Our sense of humor ranges beyond jokes, beyond wit, beyond laughter itself," and declares that "Humor, in the essence we are about to pursue, is a frame of mind, a manner of perceiving and experiencing life." He dedicates individual chapters to the effects of humor in liberating us from conformity, inferiority, morality, reason, language, naivete, redundancy (the enemy of human vitality), seriousness, and egotism.

I would be remiss in our pursuit of "What makes one worth $8,000 an hour," if I didn't pause to cite the compatibility between humor, creativity, and leadership. In all three, there is a requirement to recognize the inevitability of inconsistency, uncertainty, and being out of control. There is also a requirement to not only develop a tolerance, but an appreciation for all three in order to be successfully humorous in our approach, creative in our application, and effective in our ability to lead. Studies repeatedly demonstrate that humor boosts productivity and is a vital management tool. And Ladies Home Journal continues to cite "their husbands sense of humor" as the number one reason for falling in love, according to a polling of their readers.

In response to the question, where does this sixth sense come from? Rejoice in the fact that its innate, possessed at the time of birth in all of us, complimenting spontaneity and curiosity. Ironically, all three traits seem to be evident in effective leaders; humor, spontaneity, and curiosity. For those academics who struggle with such simplicity, please invest your research time and dollars in deciphering which came first, or better yet, if innate, what happens to it?

Whenever I express this thesis, that one's sense of humor is present at birth, I reflect back on an experience many years ago in Vietnam. As most U.S. Marines I was dedicated and true to the red, white, and blue in my allegiance and discipline to our commitment in Vietnam. I felt comfortable with my limited knowledge of precisely why it was we were there, but not overly concerned. It never really occurred to me that it was up to me to determine the appropriateness of the mission. Like many others I was comfortable with my own patriotic justification for serving. In my case, we were there to preserve what was essential for a democracy, and play a role in providing the same for a country that had been deprived of such opportunities for hundreds of years. Certainly, part of that was the freedom to be who, or what, one wanted to be. And to enjoy all that life has, and not be restricted by some socialist standards that would regulate happiness and opportunity.

I recall early in my stay "in country," when we stopped our patrol for a midday dining commonly referred to as c-rations. Having consumed this gastric feast, we casually discarded our tin cans among the children of the village, much to their delight. I later learned of some unpleasant uses for the discarded cans, but this was not the case that day. Due to the heat of the midday sun, we lounged among the shade of the trees until late afternoon. During this time, as I listened to the unrestricted laughter of children among the trees, I witnessed more joy and enthusiasm, and creativity in the use of those cans by those Vietnamese children than I had ever experienced back home in the U.S.A.

I found this to be very disturbing. After all, we were there to liberate these children and make it possible for them to experience the joys of life and freedom. How dare they have such a good time playing stick hockey with branches found along the road and tin cans discarded by some of Uncle Sam's finest. This was most unsettling.

Years later, as I began to research in earnest the origins of humor and its relationship to spontaneity and curiosity, I realized the value of that particular experience. It occurred to me that no one had to tell those children they had a right to all the joys of living. No one had to encourage them to be curious or spontaneous with their creativity due to limited resources. It was all there. It was natural, it was obvious, it was an innate sense, existing regardless of circumstances.

During public presentations when I relay this insight, pertaining to the origin of humor and its relationship to spontaneity and curiosity, I frequently hear from the skeptic among us. My principal response is, "Show me a child without spontaneity or curiosity, and I'll show you a child without a sense of humor."

As a note I should add, when we later did bring the Vietnamese refugees to California, I was not surprised to hear the children were not immediately gratified, regardless of the accessibility of three-wheelers, nintendos, and video arcades. Unfortunately, they were beginning the slow process of social orientation (U.S. style), which includes an acute awareness of the need for "things" in order to be happy. This enlightenment or dependency on "things," carries with it, a very negative consequence pertaining to future growth, development, and one's ability to enjoy life to its fullest: a diminished sense of spontaneity and curiosity. Why?

SECTION 15

HUMOR. WHAT HAPPENED TO IT?

Is it our dependency on "things" that is so damaging to our own spontaneity, curiosity, sense of humor and ultimately our earning power? Not in total, however this dependency on "things" is a critical player in contributing to a diminished belief that the answers lay within oneself. What are the other factors that contribute to this gradual erosion of ones' self?

Enemy number one. Parents! Perhaps we should have taken note of Dan Quayle's warning about the importance of the family unit. As the later Newsweek cover acknowledges, Dan Quayle Was Right! No other factor will be as significant in the overall development of the individual psyche as the parents. They are the ones with the initial exposure and the life enduring influence on us. The most commonly cited culprits in this day of victimization-the parents. "Anyone who defines himself as a victim has found a way to keep himself in a perpetual state of righteous self-pity and anger," according to Julius Lester. Parents will continue to shoulder the responsibility for their contribution to our plight.

If we attempt to minimize the impact of the parents and the home environment on the development of the individual psyche, we need to look no further than the nightly newscast to be reminded. However, more poignant may be the innocent comments that come from the youth who are experiencing the home environment, and parental influence, during their formative years.

The Minneapolis Star Tribune runs a column periodically entitled; "mindworks," reproducing essay submissions from students in grades one through 12. One can almost feel the molding of the individual as captured by their response to the topic: "Describe the kind of adult you want to become. Which traits of the adults you know do you want to possess? Which ones don't you?" Note the contrasting influences in home atmosphere and parental influence.

> I don't have that many positive role models in my life, if any. I want to be the exact opposite of my parents.
>
> They're selfish and cold-hearted. My house isn't a love-filled house. The words "I love you" are rarely, if ever, used when it comes to me or my sister. When I'm an adult I will be generous with compliments and show love and affection in every way I can. I won't be lazy or pushy. I also won't be too eager in getting rid of someone. I'll give them a chance.
>
> When I'm an adult, I want to [be]the way I wish my parents were.
>
> -Girl/Grade 7

> One thing my father never did was expect more than I could put forward. He always expected me to do the best that was possible for me, not my brothers and not the class brain. Knowing this helped me to achieve more than I ever thought possible. By his believing in me to do my best, it made me want to please him, to let him be proud of his son.
>
> I want to be as good a person as my father. By doing this I will accomplish three main things. First, maybe one day my son or

daughter will think as well of me as I do of him or her. Second, it would make my father proud if his son was as good a person as he could be. Finally, overall I will have a better life if I live like he lives.

I love my father!

-Boy/Age 15/Grade 10

"By far, the most observed and influential of adults are mothers and fathers. Most of the young people passionately described the traits they love in their parents, ranging from their willingness to listen patiently to helping them with serious problems such as bulimia. They wrote equally passionately about the traits they detest, such as impatience and bossiness.

Hundreds said they're deeply disturbed, and sometimes frightened, by adults' short tempers. When they're adults, some said, they never want to blow up so quickly and explosively."

Many said their parents spend too little time with them. One 15-year-old described the consequences of seriously negligent parents. He wrote, "I want to be there when my kids need me because my parents weren't there for me and my brother. My brother killed himself. I got heavy into drugs. I want to help my kids make the right decisions so they don't end up dead or in jail."

A significant message to all of us was conveyed by a young lady of 13. "I'm around adults every day. They probably don't even know it, but I watch them: what they do, how they do things, how they talk, just the way they act...."

Others were more basic in their observations and comments. One indicated, "They'll be the kind of adult, who will buy at least one item from every child who comes door-to-door selling something and will never make kids sing for their Halloween candy. They'll never ask the kids to clean up the dog poop."

Note, the perceived gradual erosion of the adult spirit, that is readily observable by the youngster. "I hope I never do what so many adults have done. Many adults have lost something very important, somewhere between taking their first steps and stepping their way out into the world, they've lost their dreams."

Dreams rely on curiosity. Which dies first as a result of parental influence: the dreams, the curiosity, the spontaneity, or the sense of humor?

Enemy number two. Peers. Individuals who are products of home environments that are not supportive at best, and detrimental at worst, are numerous as adults fighting the uphill-battle. Assuming the worse case scenario, the non-supportive home environment has, in all likelihood, stifled the development of the individual traits of spontaneity, curiosity, and creativity to a considerable degree. Recognizing that future earning power is directly related to ones' ability to communicate effectively, and indirectly influenced by ones sense of humor, this is not a pretty picture.

As we have previously discussed, ones' sense of humor, and ability to be receptive to others and their ideas is dependent upon, or strongly influenced, by the presence of spontaneity and curiosity. The presence of these factors, is in proportion to the extent of parental support, and non-judgmental stimulation provided in the home environment. Regardless of the level of support, or lack thereof, enemy number two, the peer group will take precedence.

The emergence of the peer group, like the home environment, presents a mixed message. On the one hand if the child emerges from a supportive home environment, and receives acceptance from a peer group which is reflective of those values previously instilled, the exposure and identification will most likely be positive. On the other hand, if the peer group extending the hand of acceptance is one in which the established norms are not held in high esteem, an internal conflict will emerge. Unfortunately, at this stage of development the peer group will usually have more influence than that of the parents.

Exactly when the parental influence yields to that of the peer group cannot be established precisely. Psychologist have argued this point of separation for decades and will continue to do so into the distant future. What they can agree on, is that the peer influence does occur, and also that the parental influence will always remain to some degree, be it positive or negative.

Enemy number three. Society. At the same time the individual is navigating through the intricacies of the home environment and parental influence, and the peer group the third enemy is mounting an almost insurmountable influence on the individuals' development. The previously mentioned influences pale in comparison to the overwhelming influence of society and its mandate to conform. Unfortunately, conformity is the antithesis of creativity and spontaneity. A major dilemma, for those who aspire for greatness, in the creative or monetary sense.

Research shows that creativity is doused by; needing to perform on demand, being pressured by excessive competition, being motivated by extrinsic vs. intrinsic rewards, and conventional "We've always done it that way thinking." Sounds a lot like conformity, doesn't it?

"Creativity begins with the right attitude: openness, flexibility, a willingness to see new ideas. Cultivating this attitude is no easy task, especially in a society that has been quietly removing it from you all your life," according to Susan Goodman.

Please note, the similarity between Goodman's prerequisites for creativity, and the definition of humor we have utilized throughout this book. Also noteworthy is what Goodman cites as being detrimental to creativity i.e. society. There is a striking similarity between what is recognized to be detrimental to creativity i.e. society, and what has previously been cited as "enemies to the emergence of humor;" i.e. parental support and home environment, peer group, and the overall process of socialization. "Society attacks early, when the individual is helpless," according to B.F. Skinner.

Given the involuntary influence of one's home environment and the inevitable influence of socialization; What is the likelihood of emerging unscathed, and receptive to others and their ideas? Not much!

Therein lies the explanation as to why few people ever reach their full potential, few maximize their earning power, and few realize the fully actualized life as portrayed by Maslow in his hierarchy of needs. Society works against us every step of the way!

Enemy number three-society, has a step-child. That child evolves as a result of a joint effort or combined influence of parents, peers, and societal pressures. The step-child that hinders our willingness to continue to be spontaneous is the ultimate "F" word, failure.

As a culture we have an extremely low tolerance for failure. Losing is taboo in our society. As Bill Ecenbarger of the Philadelphia Inquirer so blatantly states in his article; Born to Lose, "Hundreds of books have been written on how to win, scarcely any on how to lose."

Ecenbarger cautions, "Children returning from games are asked whether they won or lost, when they should be asked whether they had fun?" Have we forgotten that losers changed the world? Philadelphia Phillies pitcher, Mitch Williams appeared to have it in perspective when he responded to his poor performance in the World Series. "There shouldn't be tears. I mean, a ball game is a ball game . . . winning or losing a ball game-that's just the nature of the game." Reality: Forty days later, Williams was traded to Houston.

At some point we interrupt the sought after journey of upward mobility. Consistent with pop theories of explanation, we are all victims. Victims of our parentage, environment, or of a society which doesn't recognize our worth (hourly or annually). And if I fully believed that, this book would end at this point. Together, we could throw up our hands in righteous indignation of the hand that we were dealt with. Poor me.

To those who seek the route most frequently traveled, I bid you adieu, and appreciate that you stuck with us this long. You now have justification as to why you do not make $8,000 an hour. It appears that those individuals who make obscene salaries (12% greater than mine), are gifted with the ability to communicate effectively. Much of their effectiveness stems from their sense of humor. This sixth sense allows them to diffuse conflict, and move forward.

These prosperous individuals are compensated handsomely for their efforts. Fortunately for them, they were raised in very supportive environments. Their parents encouraged their spontaneity and curiosity, which in turn caused their creativity to flourish. Their peer groups were continually supportive of them, and not jealous or envious of their progress. They were able to traverse the socialization process unfettered. I DON'T THINK SO!

The incongruity of the above confession, becomes evident when the lives of "successful" individuals are examined. Frequently, they have overcome obstacles far more detrimental to those encountered by the average individual. This may be terribly motivational to some, and exceedingly discouraging to others. To acknowledge the hardships experienced by many successful people undermines the inconvenience of our own lives.

Bear in mind, the entrepreneur Lido Anthony Iacocca, to whom we have referred to earlier as drawing an annual income equivalent to $8,000 an hour, is the same person who grew up in depression poverty in Allentown, Pa. In his teens he was crippled with rheumatic fever, and classified 4-F by the military. He felt rejected by his country.

The danger of drawing attention to the earlier hardships of successful people, is that it may encourage those of us who did come from favorable circumstances, to seek adversity in order to justify our anticipated future success. That phenomenon is not as strange as it sounds.

When examining the self-destructive behaviors of individuals who have excelled in their respective fields; "The universal factor is the lack of self-esteem, according to clinical psychologist Mildred S. Lerner." Thus, some of the behaviors of accomplished individuals like Michael Jackson, Mike Tyson, Tonya Harding, Shannen Doherty, Woody Allen and more recently Rodman of the Bullets, become understandable.

Dr. Wayne Myers, professor of clinical psychiatry at Cornell University Medical Center in New York City added, "The classic explanation is that these people can't allow themselves to achieve success. The success is equated with something forbidden, which they feel they don't deserve. Unconsciously, they're trying to destroy their own success."

As artist, they tend to be self-destructive in public ways. "As performers they're always working for public approval," said Barbara Koltuv, a clinical psychologist and Jungian analyst in New York. "That's why they need to self-destruct in front of an audience." The "impostor phenomenon," is a popular malaise afflicting many who experience upward mobility. Simply stated, it is the belief that one will eventually be "found out." Fully aware of one's own inadequacies, life becomes a living "time bomb" waiting to be detonated. Daily newspapers are replete with those who self-detonate, or who are exposed due to investigative reporting. Recent technology, and its ability to retrieve the past, has done little to appease the anxiety of those who are afflicted.

For those who maintain the belief that the "successful," are born with the "silver spoon," I would strongly advise them to read any of the Chicken Soup for the Soul sequence by Canfield, Hansen and McNamara and be inspired as those who listen to Paul Harvey's, The Rest of the Story radio segment. As a closing thought relating to the societal enemies that restrict the growth of our spontaneity, curiosity and sense of humor, I reflect on my own experience, as a father of seven children. They have been a gold mine in availing themselves to my theories of maturation as they experience the aging process.

Much to my chagrin, they have not been able to avoid the "unintentional" hang ups of their parents, nor the influence of the peers, and the societal pressure to conform. We have worked diligently, to encourage a spirit of curiosity, the joy of spontaneity, and the satisfaction derived from creativity. The only difference between myself, as a researcher with a vested interest in discouraging the socialization process, and every other parent in this society, is I may have had the opportunity to more accurately detect the exact date of departure from spontanity, and creativity.

For the first five years of life, for our eldest child, I cherished the creative works of art, reassuring him that there may be dogs that have wheels, and cars with wings. Reviewing his drawing of a tree completed early during the fall of his kindergarten year, I asked him to explain the contribution he brought home. It was a multicolored tree with a variety of colored balls in the foliage, and similar colored balls of color laying at the base of the tree, obviously representative of a fall landscape. He explained it as such.

He further indicated that each student was called on to briefly explain their artistic rendition of a tree. When I inquired what his comments to the class were, he responded he had none. When called on, he told the teacher he hadn't done a drawing. Why? The five classmates who had preceded him, all had contributed a more traditional drawing of a tree, complete with round fluff-ball of green foliage on top. His perception was, that his drawing was too distinct, and thus prone to the ridicule of his classmates. The transition of an individual spirit was in process.

I attempted my parental endorsement of creativity, and all the related psych-babble about the importance of individuality, however his glazed over look conveyed the reality, that he would probably do the same, given another opportunity. The acceptance by his peers, was replacing any rewards derived from his own individuality, or praise from his father. I can pinpoint the exact day I was struck with this truism.

On another occasion, I was struck by evidence of the socialization process. The school district in which we reside, has a day called, activity day. On this specific day students are given the opportunity to try a variety of experiences in order to expand their horizons. They select which activities they desire from a comprehensive listing provided. I was pleased with my son's inquiring mind, when he brought the listing home in seventh grade. According to him the only prerequisite for selection was, "something he hadn't done before." He ended up with class sessions in macrame, cooking, and folk dancing. He had a most enjoyable day.

The next year, the only self-imposed prerequisite for selection? Which classes are my friends going to attend? Welcome to the world of the peer group.

My wife and I have replayed the above scenario countless times, wondering what we could have done differently to instill a greater degree of self-confidence in our son. We contemplated counseling, until we looked into the cost, and they we settled for reality. Our son would be no different, than every other child in this society. There was no way we could protect him from the process, and the consequences of socialization. The best we can do as parents is to model the values and principles we desire in our children.

As to the other six siblings following in his wake, we have "chilled." I am no longer devastated by their overwhelming desire "to fit in, and be perfect." We take in stride the reality of the process, knowing to leave the house in something less than; an appropriately signatured backpack, FUBU shirt, and baggy pants boarders on anarchy.

When I attempt to convince my wife that I was never a conformist, I was an independent, free to move about without the shackles of imitation, she makes a valid observation. I have been wearing my hair the same for thirty-five years. Why? I like the way it looked on James Darren!

SECTION 16

DECISIONS AND CONSEQUENCES

Twenty years ago, when I began my pursuit of the "mysterious trait," that separates the stars from the also-rans, the journey appeared complete with the realizations articulated in the previous chapter. The possession of a keen sense of humor was the "mysterious trait," essential to success. I pursued the talk circuit, confident that my findings would provide comfort to all seeking upward mobility. Meaningful examples of individuals who effectively used humor to advance their cause were plentiful, thanks to the advent of videotape, and the ubiquitous influence of CNN. Ronald Reagan was heaven sent, and daily demonstrated his ability to defuse conflict with the use of humor.

The progression became clear; a sense of humor, present at birth, influences a "childlike demeanor," complete with spontaneity and curiosity. This sixth sense is manifested in a personality which is receptive to others and their ideas, thus enhancing a creative spirit.

This receptiveness to others, becomes very predictable, and expected, radiating a spirit of warmth that is sought and envied by all.

This charismatic shield, provides insulation from undesired criticism, as well as serving as an offensive safeguard for advancing one's agenda, with limited resistance.

The recognition of the natural enemies, to developing one's sense of humor; parents, peers, and the socialization process removed all mystique from this mysterious trait. The secret is now known to all. On numerous occasions, I ended my presentation once I had revealed the origin of the trait that is so critical to ones success, and the obstacles, which will impede its development. The case was solved.

Audiences were quick to acknowledge the significance of my findings, and were quick to applaud the relevance of the examples which I had captured in text, slides, and videotape. Finally, there was an explanation, which fully accounted for the limited success, and subsequent envy of individual audience members.

This realization also provided an explanation for a number of unrelated social phenomenon which are troublesome. The public fascination with celebrities, tabloids, television, movie stars, talk shows, horoscopes, and the supernatural, became more clear. There appears to be a correlation with one's willingness to accept one's plight in life, and one's willingness to be a spectator in life opposed to being fully involved.

This spectator mentality appears to be in direct conflict with the natural instincts, which are inherent at birth. What happened? Somewhere, sometime, in the developmental process we determined it was easier, or more rewarding to experience the path travelled by others, than to brave our own way. In essence, we yield part of ourselves to the control of others. The part that we are releasing to the influence of others is the part that makes us truly unique. It is also the part that is instrumental in contributing to our future success, not only in monetary terms, which no doubt are affected, but creative terms, due to our willingness to yield our spontaneity and curiosity. For the most part this is done at the subconscious level.

As competitors, or in a less confrontational manner as participants, we do not consciously sit down and say, "From here on out, I will cease to be a formidable challenge to my peers." The transition is far more subtle, but nevertheless as detrimental. How early, or when does this take place? Exact time of transformation would vary with each person, however not by much. I would submit, as soon as one realizes there are benefits to be had by "conforming," the metamorphosis has begun. Certainly, the early parental influences would have considerable impact, at the latest, transition would start with the introduction of formalized education, and continue for the balance of our lives.

Bloom examines the influence of this desire to conform in his appropriately titled book; The Closing of the American Mind, which examines the last quarter of a century in higher education. In spite of countless research that proclaims the value of hands on, small group interaction, and the use of technology in the classroom, the vast majority of classes plod along utilizing outdated memorization and lecture techniques. This approach challenges the student to retain the information until the quarterly quiz, with limited emphasis on one's ability to think creatively. Why does education continue to do that? If one accepts the premise of the previous paragraph, the answer is apparent. Present teachers are not immune to the socialization process, and unfortunately have emerged from an educational system that offers limited rewards to those who venture out of the "tried but true" approach to education. What you see, is what they saw!

At approximately the same time we begin to yield our own judgement over to the dictates of society, another struggle seems to occur. There is a constant internal conflict which rears its ugly head. The conflict is one of choice. We are repeatedly confronted with what is intellectually best for us, versus what is emotionally pleasurable to us. Again, the specific chronological time of the conflict occurring varies in each of us, but not by much. Suffice it to say that this struggle follows the first choice of sacrificing our own judgement to some other entity. There is a need to have developed a degree of mental competency in order to allow one the capacity to distinguish what is intellectually "best" in a given situation.

Our institutions are filled with individuals who never transgress beyond this struggle. Their careers are filled with decisions that are influenced by another's' judgement, and constantly do what "feels good" opposed to what is in their best interest. Ironically, when given an opportunity to reflect on their obdurate ways, it is the rare individual who accepts responsibility, however the villain (society), is quickly identified. Those individuals are not the concern of this book. This book relates to those individuals who are cognizant of some of the poor decisions they have made, however, are not willing to accept defeat at the hands of society. Yet!

In The Celestine Prophecy, Redfield is quick to point out how discernable our journey through life has been. What appeared to be coincidences at the time, emerge as milestones aided by the perspective of reflection. Those events, in particular, those which were guided by the judgement of others', or emotional in nature, and subsequently detrimental to our development, become glaring.

I am tempted to insert three blank pages at this point, suggesting the reader record those "glaring" events which have been so instrumental in contributing to their current situation. Or as Redfield said, "Your whole life has been a long road leading directly to this moment." I might also add that this thought, of inserting blank pages, was one of emotional origin, and was quickly brought back in check by the intellectual reality that such an exercise may cause a good percentage of the readership to discontinue reading, and seek therapy. Don't despair, help is pages away.

A third dynamic, happening simultaneously with our struggle to trust our own judgement or the judgement of others', and the choice to go with what is intellectually sound or emotionally inviting, is our choice to maintain a sharp mental focus or to drift.

Unfortunately, our psychological development does not parallel our educational progression through life. There is not a convenient categorization similar to grades K-6, middle school, high school, college, and graduate school to which we can refer our psychological development. An advanced degree assures a certain maturity in a given area of expertise, from there on, it's a crap shoot.

It is not possible to segment isolated periods when we yield to our judgement, or our intellect to the dictates of society. Nor, is it possible to isolate precisely, when we are allowing our minds to drift, opposed to being focused. There certainly is an element of drift at play when we trust another's judgment over our own, and when we gravitate toward what is momentarily pleasurable opposed to what is intellectually sound over the long run.

There is also difficulty determining what is mental drift, opposed to what is a sharply focused mind. The confusion exists because some activities that are clearly "drift," may be intellectually appropriate given a specific set of circumstances. The example that comes to mind, is watching television. To flop down in front of the television, complete with bag of pretzels and a cold one, at the completion of a week's work (TGIF), may be very appropriate. However, to flop and channel surf ad nauseam on a nightly bases, displays somewhat of a mindless drift, and certainly yields to the emotional temptation within all of us.

It is the preponderant influence, and acceptance, of this drifting lifestyle that eventually leads us to believe that we are no longer in control, or more importantly "worthy," of more. This conclusion is devastating to our psyche, and ultimate to our development. At this time, we complete another transformation in life. We assent to the life of a "spectator," in contrast to that of a life of a "participant." Our fulfillment begins to come from our knowledge and awareness of the accomplishments of others. "I may not be able to play, but I can tell you the starting lineup, and the designated hitter on each team." There is a point where this expertise amongst our peers, begins to take on the same degree of significance as when we actually played!

This parasitic existence is in such contrast to where we began as children; fully aware, fully stimulated, and fully involved. The comparison is most unsettling. Our knowledge of prominent celebrities and the gossip that accompanies them, begins to take precedent over our own development. Our ability to converse about the possible pairings for the pennant race, begins to take on an importance greater than that of our own evolution. Our existence becomes secondary to our knowledge of another's' welfare. Something has gone amuck. However, to ask or inquire too diligently, would require focus, intellect, and certainly a judgement that would not be supported by our contemporaries. How stifling would it be in the midst of discussing the possible combinations for the upcoming Super Bowl, someone yells out, who cares! Please.

If one were capable of taking a quick snapshot in time, what would the self-portrait mirror? Would it reflect an individual who is emotionally adrift, for all practical purposes, dependent on the whims of society to determine his destiny, and trusting others to determine what is best for him. Armed with this realization, and aware of what has previously been revealed in this book, would they be able to turn back the clock, and remold the person that presently exists? The answer is yes, but it would require a great deal of effort, and the reader should be aware of the trappings, as well as the rewards associated with this journey back in time.

At first blush the individual who has decided to "take charge" of his life should be encouraged to begin the journey immediately. In reality, this journey is an extension of the present, leading directly to some future moment in time. Hypothetically, the individual who decides, as of this moment, to be focused, no longer drifting; intellectual, no longer emotional; and trusting of his own judgement, opposed to that of others; will be on the road to recovery and prosperity.

Unfortunately, the demons that usually accompany quick weight loss, and subsequent weight return, are present with abrupt changes in our psychic makeup. The return of weight, does not depend as much on caloric content, as it does on mental preparation. This would explain why most reputable diets stress a slow gradual loss, opposed to quick drastic change. What is hidden in that advice is an assumption that one matures mentally inversely, to the weight lost. The two must happen simultaneously. A head trip, at the same time as the body trip, and both requiring sufficient time and opportunity to adjust. If one trip accelerates too rapidly, it will be at the expense of the other. The reason for this is evolutionary in concept.

As developing individuals, our self-worth is dependent upon the preponderance of decisions that we have made that are beneficial to us, versus the number of decisions which we have made that are not. Eventually our lives begin to be reflective of this sequence. In a very elementary observation, it appears that good things continue to repeatedly happen to certain individuals, and the undesirable consequences of life continue to plague another segment of society.

This may appear as an over simplification, therefore in an effort to, make it meaningful, one must examine his own life.

According to Dr. Maxwell Maltz, author of Psycho-Cybernetics, "A person's behavior is always consistent with {their} self-image." If a person carries the self-image of failure, he will find some way to fail despite his good intentions, If, on the other hand, a person sees himself as victorious, he will find some way to succeed despite the presence of obstacles.

Frequently, those individuals who are experiencing upward mobility, are very focused, confident in their own judgement, and emotionally strung out. A closer examination may reveal financial stability, and good health both physically and spiritually. In contrast, individuals who are experiencing employment difficulties over an extended period of time, are frequently somewhat adrift and dependent upon the opinions of others to set direction in their own life. A closer examination may also reveal an over extension financially and a less than desirable state of health both physically and spiritually.

Admittedly, there is great difficulty in taking this exaggerated example to extremes in order to make a point. We can all identify individuals, ourselves included, who manifest some of the traits represented, but not all, in order to conform to the stereotype as represented. The point is, there is something more at work that accounts for the overall consistency in one's lifestyle, than mere coincidence.

In order to understand the dynamic at work, we reference the work of Nathaniel Branden. His contributions; The Psychology of Self-Esteem, The Disowned Self, and Breaking Free are instrumental in explaining why it so frequently appears that people either, have it together, or they don't.

I utilized Branden's work while a faculty member at Northern Michigan University. At the time I was an instructor with the Department of Criminal Justice, and spent countless hours seeking an answer to what makes criminals do what they do. Or what can Charles Manson do for contemporary management?

We incorporated Branden's work in a course entitle; Treatment of the Offender. Like most instructors, I did a thorough review of his work prior to assigning the text as mandatory reading for the class. Which is another way of saying, I liked the title and read the dust-jacket. To quote Branden; "The central theme of this book is the role of self-esteem in man's life: the need of self-esteem, the nature of that need, the conditions of its fulfillment, the consequences of its frustration-and the impact of a man's self esteem (or lack of it), on his values, responses and goals." That certainly sounded as if it were on target to me!

With the required nightly reading assigned to the students, we began to wade through part one which deals with the "foundations" of psychology as a science and ultimately its importance to one's mental health. By mid-semester, I was facing a mutiny by some very impatient students, who were making some wild accusations regarding my competencies. Unfortunately, I had to agree. It was pretty tough going to begin with. In order to maintain any degree of professional stature, I assured the students "It gets better as you get into it." I hurriedly raced home to read the next chapter to determine if there was anything salvageable. I must admit, there was.

According to Branden, one's self esteem is dependent upon the choices (volitions) one makes, pertaining to the three internal struggles we have previously mentioned:

1. To maintain a sharp mental focus, or to drift;
2. To exercise one's intellect or emotion;
3. To trust one's own judgement, or the judgement of others'.

An individuals' self-esteem is molded or influenced by the above three major decision opportunities that present themselves repeatedly throughout the day, and ultimately throughout one's life. How one responds to these opportunities will ultimately determine one's self-confidence and self-esteem. The above three opportunities are not necessarily mutually exclusive. They frequently appear together and reinforce one another. In response to; "Where do you want to go for lunch?" one responds; "I don't care, just drive," all three opportunities are being violated. The response is one of drift, emotion, and trusting of someone else's judgement.

The above example is offered in order to make a point, not to suggest, that one's psyche will be permanently damaged if they are indecisive regarding where to go for lunch. What is suggested is that our lives are comprised of a multitude of similar situations, each requiring us to make a choice, usually reflective of one of the three, or a combination of the three dynamics mentioned.

A preponderance of negative choices, or negative choices pertaining to significant opportunities in life will eventually be damaging to one's development. Some of these "significant" opportunities may begin very early in life. The selection of a peer group comes to mind. If a child is not secure in who he wants as peers, he most likely will go with the individual or group which is most receptive of him. A decision like this, which on the surface, may be dismissed as "adjusting" may be critical in its influence as to which direction that child eventually journeys.

Shift the opportunity in the above example to the parent of the child seeking "adjustment". At the same time the child is seeking acceptance, the parents may be bombarded with their own life circumstances pertaining to employment, social groupings etc. How the parent responds to these opportunities will directly influence the development of the child. As the parent responds to the stresses of the everyday world, his choices or volitions will modify the choices available to the child.

If the parents are preoccupied, they may be inclined to take the line of least resistance. If it becomes more convenient to pick up fast food, the child may have limited opportunity to choose or focus on what is intellectually best for him, opposed to what is the most convenient. In this situation the child's judgement has been delegated to another-the parent. The example of fast foods is used because it is one we can all associate with, and consumer studies indicate it is one of the opportunities that is most frequently sacrificed in the name of convenience. Apply the same logic to a child's study habits, bedtime, leisure activity, peer associates, organizational involvement, use of the car, curfew, and spiritual growth and one quickly realizes the degree of influence the parent has in the development of the child.

The frequency, as well as the significance of any one decision, begins to mold the personality. Assume one exercises an active role, opposed to a reactive role, and selects the positive choice the majority of the time opposed to the negative option, identified in the parentheses. The following progression may be anticipated. One is led by reason (emotion), they begin to experience a sense of control (out of control), which leads to a feeling of self-confidence (not confident). As one develops confidence, they feel competent (incompetent), and worthy (unworthy), and welcome additional challenges (safety). They are inclined to seek risk (security). The motivated individual is active (reactive), and the cycle continues to repeat itself, therefore it appears that good things continue to happen to certain individuals, and the bad things frequently continue to happen to another segment of the population. The rich get richer!

As a college instructor I distributed, "Weekend In Review" worksheets each Monday during class. I would instruct each student to reflect on his activities from 6:00 PM Friday to 6:00 AM Monday. This time frame was broken down by hourly increments. The question was; "Indicate what you did during each 60 minute interval. Do you consider that activity to be reflective of a sharp mental focus, intellectual in nature, and primarily reflective of your own judgement? Or, does that hourly activity reflect mental drift, emotion, and dependent on the judgement of another as to what is best for you?"

This was an excellent exercise in demonstrating the control that we have in molding the person whom we eventually become. The range of response was significant. For some, the response sheet was a parents dream, including part-time work, study time, socializing, exercising and relaxation. For others, it was a parents worse nightmare come true-a Friday afternoon exit to celebrate TGIF leading to a Monday AM at a remote location in the city. Specific travel, company, etc. could not be immediately identified.

Weekends were selected for this exercise to allow for the maximum amount of freedom and self-choice. Much of our week is dedicated to classes, work, and survival. The weekend becomes the true "window to the soul." What we do with our free time is critical in determining who we are.

For the twenty-year old coed, where he is emotionally, is reflective of the previous 1040 weekends lived to date. More significantly, the 52 weekends since the parental influence has been minimized due to departure from the home environment last year.

The use of the term "free time" is usually met with a great deal of hostility by those among us who have no "free time." Unfortunately, those who are most adamant about their lack of free time are experiencing some of the aftershock of lives when activities that resulted in instant gratification were the rule, rather than the exception. All behaviors have consequences, unfortunately for many this lesson becomes a reality at the most inconvenient time.

For those students who would suggest some mythical deity was in possession of their ability to reason clearly and make choices that were beneficial to them, we referred to an early work by Dr. Wayne Dyer. In his work; Your Erroneous Zones, he exposes the four favorite neurotic justifications of the American people: "THAT'S ME,' I CAN'T HELP IT,' 'I'VE ALWAYS BEEN THAT WAY,' and 'IT'S JUST MY NATURE.' For the truly Bonafede neurotic, if one listens closely he may hear all four justifications used in the same sentence, and offered as a justification for continuing the self-defeating lifestyle.

Years ago I heard an adage that we were all allocated a certain number of words to be spoken in a lifetime. When one exhausted their allotment-they died. When I reflect back on the "Weekend In Review" activity sheet, it appears that in our lives we have a predetermined number of hours for which we will not be accountable. We may expend those hours carelessly during our youth, and work diligently until our death; or we may be focused during our younger days, and enjoy a leisurely retirement. This issue deserves additional attention in the future.

If by chance, you happen to be one of these individuals who appears to be on the downward spiral, be aware we are a very resilient group. In order to survive we have a tremendous coping ability. To the individual experiencing the freedom of society, the concept of prison is a formidable thought. However, research indicates, some inmates become so adaptable, they prefer incarceration to the freedom available to a law-abiding citizen. They have become more dependent, and life becomes "self-imprisonment." Sadly, literally millions of "free" people go about their daily existence confined to the unimaginable.

This ability to cope with an inmate mentality, was demonstrated to me early in my career as a probation officer. One particular probationer was repeatedly late or absent for his monthly visit, and was making little effort to improve his current plight. He once again missed his appointment and I was convinced the only way to get through to him was revoke his probationary status and let him do some jail time.

Having been stood up once again, I went to his home approximately two miles away. It was the dead of winter and he opened the door in his undershorts and I could hear the drone of Donahue in the background. I verbalized my discontent regarding his absence earlier that morning. He indicated his car would not start, and he had no money for a bus or cab, which I suspect was probably true. He did not have a phone, nor did he have the change to make the appropriate telephone call and reschedule. Finally, out of frustration, I asked why didn't he just walk or hitchhike the two miles to my office, in order to eliminate the possibility of going to jail. He responded, he would have, but didn't have any pants to wear. That was just about the final straw, because I had seen him on other occasions, and he was obviously clothed at the time.

"Why didn't he wear the jeans that he wore during our last session?"

"Oh those. They had been burnt up in this morning's fire."

(God give me strength) "And where was this fire?"

"Outback. The garage had caught on fire, as a result of some gasoline that ignited, while he was working on the car." There was a strong hint that the repaired car, would have provided the transportation, in order to meet his probationary obligation. Sure. How dumb do I really look?

He went on to add, "The jeans were on the clothesline attached to the burning garage, they were lost in the fire also."

At this point, I could feel the blood pressure rising in anticipation of the five minutes it would take a police car to arrive and provide transportation for this pathological liar. But first:

"I'm sure you wouldn't mind if I look at the scene of the fire before we go, would you?" I offered sarcastically.

"Not at all."

He stepped outside, clad in underwear and barefoot, in frigid temperatures. He escorted me behind the old wooden framed house. There to my astonishment, still smoldering, was the charred remains of a garage, complete with a line of clothing (jeans included), still smoldering on the ground.

The memory of that morning lingers to this day. Not so much that a guy missed an appointment, was totally broke, phoneless and pant less, but that it was obvious that this day was not deemed unusual by him! Pretty much a typical, run of the mill day for him.

Later that afternoon, I went to an apartment complex of another member of my probationary caseload. There was a hole blown in the front door of his apartment the size of a coconut, and appeared to be caused by a shotgun blast. I peered inside, trying not to disturb him or his wife who were totally spellbound by reruns of Candid Camera.

On inquiry about the newly ventilated front door, he admitted he knew it was done by his neighbor, (via shotgun), living in apartment #211 of the same complex. Apparently, the neighbor was disenchanted because he suspected my client had stolen his stereo in retaliation for his earlier theft of my clients toolbox. My client denied any knowledge of the stolen stereo. He went on to explain, that he had not notified the police about the incident because he didn't want them to begin an investigation about his relationship with the neighbor who settles disputes with a shotgun. Here's the punch line. He didn't want the police involved because they may in fact, find his missing toolbox (which he didn't use), but more importantly they may find in my client's possession a fishing rod, that he had in fact stolen from his neighbor residing in #211. This discovery would have altered the ice fishing my client had anticipated for later that day.

"And, besides," he offers "No one was injured by the shotgun blast, so what harm had been done?"

That evening, I took a very long, and very hot bath, reflecting on the events of the day. That day lives in infamy for me. My day may be altered by the absence of hot water in the morning, their days are filled with events, which I have yet to develop the appropriate coping mechanisms. Granted, given a lifetime of days filled with similar adversity, my perception of life, of what I want and what I expect would change dramatically. It's all a matter of perspective.

Earlier writings were interrupted for a lunch break at the local dinner, and I was struck by an incident which took place. As I enjoyed the meal I could hear a television in the background broadcasting the proceedings of the O.J. Simpson trial. I glanced over to the Radiogram, which is a local daily flyer distributed about town. One segment of the flyer is entitled; "Today In History," and recaps events that occurred on this date previously. In addition to Napoleon divorcing Josephine on this date in 1809; in 1973 O.J. Simpson became the first running back in NFL history to rush for 2,000 yards in a season. Who could have imagined how his life would change? Who could have imagined what was really taking place in the life he lived, regardless of the outcome of the trial?

I was struck by the irony. Once a life of accomplishment, and the envy of millions. Today, an existence, envied by none. In one respect his life is analogous to our own. Our life merely reflects the decisions we have made, one incident, and one day at a time. All behavior, has consequence. Some more severe than others, and some irreversible.

Incidentally, at lunch I was also confronted with a decision that could be reflective of a life of sharp mental focus, intelligent, and one of my own doings; or a life adrift, emotional, and dependent upon the judgement of others! I passed on the pie for dessert.

There is one more dynamic at play of which the reader should be aware. I refer to it as imposter phenomenon, and Branden refers to it as pseudo self-esteem.

"So intensely does a man feel the need of a positive view of himself, that he may evade, repress, distort his judgement, disintegrate his mind in order to avoid coming face to face with facts that would affect his self-appraisal adversely. A man who has chosen or accepted irrational standards by which to judge himself, can be driven all his life to pursue flagrantly self-destructive goals in order to assure himself that he possesses a self-esteem which in fact he does not have," according to Branden.

"If and to the extent that men lack self-esteem, they feel driven to fake it, to create the illusion of self-esteem-condemning themselves to chronic psychological fraud-moved by the desperate sense that to face the universe without self-esteem is to stand naked, disarmed, delivered to destruction" according to Branden.

A firm understanding of the concept of pseudo self-esteem goes a long way in explaining why we buy cars with outrageous sticker prices, not to mention insurance; homes with more square footage than we'll ever need; clothes that make us subservient to plastic credit cards; and marry individuals to whom we are not compatible. These are choices we make that ultimately work against our well-being.

I've always been intrigued by Rabbi Kushner's suggestion that we will be accountable for only one answer on the inevitable "day of judgement:" "What have you done with all those opportunities I gave you?" Or, as more recently articulated in The Shawshank Redemption, "Get busy living or get busy dying."

SECTION 17

RESTORING INNER CONFIDENCE

We move forward with some extra baggage with the knowledge that a finely developed sense of humor is essential to upward mobility, and an awareness that our innate sense of humor may have been severely stifled along the way. Blame may be equally distributed amongst our parents, peers, and the influences of the society in which we live. We are also now cognizant of the role we have played, both consciously and subconsciously, pertaining to molding who we are today. The short cut, pseudo-self-esteem, has also been identified. Is there hope?

Rejoice in the knowledge that the past is littered with debris, but the future is as clean as new fallen snow, with unlimited opportunity to become who we want to be. How can we balance out what currently is, or undo what has been done in the past?

The secret lies in the origin of humor, and the socialization that subsequently dampens its continuation. As stated previously, we learn early in life that acceptance and approval, extends to those who conform. Our desire for acceptance, and our obsession with perfection, and our desire to fit in, creates a profusion of fears, self-condemnations, frustrations and angers that may be kept in check so that we don't exceed a neurosis that transcends one of the therapy groups available. The benefit of a therapy group may be in determining the distinctive classification or category, of "what we have," but more importantly may serve as the vehicle which identifies "who did it to us."

The jaded perception stems from the reality that a host of predators contributing to one's negative situation may be identified. Bottom line? It's up to the individual to change. If one needs the support of the group to come to this realization-attend the meeting.

According to Damian McElrath assistant to the president at the Hazelden Foundation in City Center, Minnesota, a nonprofit agency providing a range of services relating to chemical dependency; "I don't want to be critical of any movements, but I think the label of extending the idea of illness to everything conceivable is a problem. Every movement goes to extremes at times, and some of the things being labeled as illness are part of the human condition and of growing up."

Charles Sykes, author of "A Nation of Victims," said the chorus of powerlessness over one's problems has become so shrill that, "If Walt Whitman were to come back to America in the 20th century, he wouldn't hear America singing. He would hear America whining."

Jane Middleton-Moz said codependency, "Has proliferated too far," allowing its devotees to project responsibility away from themselves and to engage in unnecessary blaming. She has recognized 254 symptoms of codependency.

In "The Diseasing of America," psychologist Stanton Peele observes; "They're all at these meetings, complaining about how they were treated as children. Meanwhile their kids are at home. You wonder what groups they're going to go to when they grow up."

Perhaps the psychiatrist-and-psychologist team of Steven J. and Sybil Wolin who introduced the concept of "resiliency therapy," have reduced the issue to the most basic of explanations; "People are going to realize that to get better, you just have to change." It doesn't get any clearer than that.

What are we changing for? A recap of the previous chapters, provides the most concise answer. Previously we recognized the importance of perception as it relates to effective communication. Perception is changed by education, and new experiences.

In earlier chapters, it was demonstrated how a sense of humor is an apparent trait of successful people in our society. Our sense of humor, which we are born with has been stifled, due to the socialization process. Is it possible that individual change can counterbalance the influence of the socialization process?

Section 16 recognizes how the decisions of the past have been instrumental in influencing who, and where, we are today. If we changed our decision-making tendencies, would we influence our future destiny?

Furthermore, the reader became cognizant of how the decisions of the past have molded the perceptions of the day. Our self-concept is merely the perception we have of ourselves. Our self-esteem, is how we feel about these perceptions. Both are affected by change. If change is so instrumental in our future success, why are we so reluctant to change? Furthermore, if we are willing to change, what degree of change is necessary in order to bring about the desired success?

The first question is the easier of the two, due to the proliferation of literature available dealing with the issue, and obvious risk associated with change. We cannot become what we need to be, by remaining what we are. In our own lives "change" becomes a four-letter word. Why is this? If we revert back to earlier chapters, we realize it is no coincidence that individuals who make sound decisions (focused, intelligent, and of their own choosing), begin a progression that begins with action and ends with a willingness to take risk. Contrasted with individuals who's decisions reflecting an atmosphere of drift, emotions, and dependency on others. A life style that progresses from a "reactive" mode and culminates in a desire for security opposed to challenge and risk. "People fear change because it undermines their security." Ironically, one's future success may depend on their willingness to change and take risk.

Underlying an unwillingness to change or take risk, is the fear of failure. Two decades of study suggest there appears to be a critical variable which separates, not only the very successful from the not so successful, but more importantly those with a keenly refined sense of humor, opposed to those with a less refined or non-existent sense of humor.

Successful people do not define their own sense of worth in terms of success or failure associated with a given project or effort. Their sense of worth remains intact regardless of the outcome of a particular endeavor. Granted, much of this self-assurance stems from the socialization process and its influence on them specifically. Many times, this process has been a very positive experience. However, there has also been a maturing that is critical to recognize. Somewhere within this process of maturing, they (successful people), have realized that its okay to make a mistake, and move on. Many of us live in anxiety, with the expectation that it is not okay to make a mistake. We will hold that belief in order to justify not changing, and not taking risk that may jeopardize our current security. We become our own worst enemy.

We become very adept in articulating why we don't change or take risk. E.F. Borisch product manager at Milwaukee Gear company has gone to the trouble of identifying fifty reasons why we/it/ they/can't change. I offer the top ten according to Borisch:

1. We've never done it before;
2. Nobody else has ever done it;
3. It has never been tried before;
4. We tried it before;
5. Another company/person tried it before;
6. We've been doing it this way for 25 years;
7. It won't work in a small company;
8. It won't work in a large company;
9. It won't work in our company;
10. Why change-it's working OK.

The last justification is the one challenging every reader of this book. By virtue of reading this book, there is a strong suspicion, that the reader is not in agreement with #10. Everything is not OK. There are a lot of people making a lot more money than you, and are no sharper than you.

In addition to our fear of failure, we avoid change/risk because it requires an action or a decision. Or more importantly, if we do take action, and are successful, we may feel guilty and undeserving of the subsequent success (as mentioned previously in the self-destructive behaviors of celebrities etc.). Success means we may be the target of envy or alienation from our peers, who have chosen to remain on a more predictable journey through life.

Let's pause. As a reader if you can review the above paragraph and acknowledge that you are not willing to take a risk that will require an action or decision, or willing to separate from the security of your peer group, you should quit reading and pass this book on to an associate who wants to reach for the unreachable. If we are to perceive all the implications of the new, we must risk, at least temporarily, ambiguity and disorder.

Jinx Milea author of "Why Jenny Can't Lead," offers the following, "One of the best lessons children learn through video games is standing still will get them killed quicker than anything else." Tom Peters cautions; "Constant change by everyone requires a dramatic increase in the capacity to accept disruption." The dean of the Sloan School of Management, gives the following option; "A competitive world has two possibilities for you. You can lose. Or if you want to win, you can change." Perhaps the most profound insight was offered by Thoreau more than a century ago; "Things do not change; we change.

American essayist, Ralph Waldo Emerson reflects, "It was a high counsel that I once heard given to a young person, "Always do what you are afraid to do." In a conference setting most in attendance interpret this advice to mean "skydive." Fortunately, I have learned over the years that this sort of conclusion usually adds justification #51 to Borisch's justifications of why we shouldn't change. Emerson's advice is sound, however must be narrowed in order to retain the audience, and meet the need.

Risk is essential in order to move forward. The "success" or "lack thereof", as a result of the risk is of little consequence. It is the mere engagement of risk that provides the benefit. The benefit is cutting through the socialization that has occurred to date. A willingness to become, someone other than who society has dictated we become. The significance is not in taking the risk, the significance is what it does to us mentally, to step outside of the pathway as designed by "society."

If one were to endorse contemporary research Emerson's challenge, to do what we fear most, would be met by requiring "public speaking," (the #1 fear of the American public), for everyone. This fear is greater than the #2 fear, the fear of death, and by inference we may conclude the #3 fear, the fear of dying while giving a public speech. Life is not so simplistic. I would welcome the opportunity to give a public speech, however the thought of skydiving makes me seek refuge. What is most risky or freighting, is a very individualistic issue, and usually not shared.

In "Repacking Your Bags: Lighten Your Load for the Rest of Your Life," authors Richard Leider and David Shapiro write, "We've discovered that many people are laboring through their lives, weighted down by attachments that no longer serve them." Included in those fears are: fear of having lived a meaningless life, fear of being alone, fear of being lost, and the fear of death.

It is the act of defiance, of going against what society has dictated, that is essential to our development. The development may in fact be at the subconscious level, but it serves as the catalyst for the emergence of one's sense of humor, the essential ingredient to effective communication, and upward mobility. The degree of risk, is another issue.

My earlier experience as a correctional worker has been a tremendous asset in developing insight relating to "an appropriate" degree of risk in which an individual might engage in order to experience upward mobility. In developing treatment plans for probationers and parolees, most caseworkers make the same mistake. In the proposed "treatment section" for the client the most popular recommendations are; complete dependency program, gain a educational degree, and maintain gainful employment. All three of these require a degree of educational preparation beyond the imagination of the typical offender. All require, a discipline and allegiance to a philosophy to which the majority of inmates have never been exposed, or in the case of exposure, the experience has been negative.

Most treatment plans require basic abilities such as the ability to read and write, frequently not traits of the incarcerated. All require a level of perseverance, and dedication. Traits if present, would have gone a long way toward preventing criminal participation in the first place. But more critically, the basic belief in one's ability to succeed is the major obstacle to offender rehabilitation. For the most part, the incarcerated individual has no concept of what it is to succeed in organized, acceptable socially endorsed activities. Therein lies the challenge to the caseworker.

Given the above profile, what could one suggest that would contribute to an offenders' success, and begin the long road to resourcefulness? A popular first step for effective caseworkers is teaching the client how to use the telephone. The skills required for directory assistance is a popular second step. Notice the use of the telephone book comes much later. Issues pertaining to personal hygiene, are usually a major focus during the first year of adjustment. Once a degree of individual "freedom" and selfdetermination is established, the weighted goals of "the rights and freedoms of others," may be bridged. It is a very slow, tedious, and usually painful process. Dr. Maxwell Maltz admonition warrents repeated, "A person's behavior is always consistent with his self-image."

How does the world of inmates transfer to useful information to the citizenry at large. The example is offered in order to provide perspective. Just as one cannot impose inappropriate risk related challenges on inmates, the challenges presented to readers should not exceed their grasp at the beginning of the development period. The overriding goal is not to conquer an existing fear or vanquish a present risk. The goal is to experience the joy, and new found freedom that emerges from taking control, and giving oneself two basic freedoms: the permission to be someone greater than who society has said you should be, and secondly the freedom to fail. This applies to all risk except skydiving, where it is essential that one be right the first time.

In practical application, this translates to the most minute challenge or risk imaginable, comparable to being able to dial information (in your own area code). At conferences, ask participants to get up and greet one another with the high ten (an expansion to the high five), and give out a yell. Then sit back and listen to what happens when the childlike spontaneity that has lain dormant is given permission to come forth.

There is a child within all of us, that yearns to be free. To live and enjoy who and what we are, and anxiously awaits the challenges and opportunities of the day. What happened to this enthusiasm we had for life? Nothing. It just got buried in the socialization process along the way. It longs to be awakened. Coinciding with that awakening process, is the emergence of that trait so critical to our success and mobility, our willingness to be receptive to others and their opinions, complete in the literal sense of the word-our sense of humor.

What is the appropriate risk, or degree of challenge? Only one person can determine that. You. It varies with all of us, as does our tolerance for failure. I would merely caution, that as one determines which risk to take, one should also stay focused, on what is intellectually sound, legal, and not detrimental to ones' health, and most importantly trusting in your judgement. That leaves a lot of room to maneuver!

It is inevitable, when presenting this challenge, "Take a risk", to conferees, there is a multitude who are totally stymied by what they should do that would constitute a risk. When examined closely, that immediate impasse, is a societal indictment of what has been expressed in these pages. We become so dependent on our culture to provide us direction as to who, or what we should be, when challenged to do virtually anything, we are at an impasse. Unfortunately, even this look of forbearance, is predictable.

Immediately, the reality that one should never suggest what an appropriate risk for another is, is reviewed. If we ask another to identify an appropriate risk for ourselves, we are violating another tenet of positive self-esteem, and yielding our judgement over to another, as to what is best for us.

For those who are truly stymied, it is pointed out that participation in a class or activity that may expand one's imagination would certainly seem to be appropriate, given their bewildered response to the challenge. It is the rare child, possessing an innate curiosity and spontaneity, that wanders about aimlessly, when given unlimited freedom. However, our children quickly learn, that a little whining goes a long way. The parent who quickly responds to the child who whines by providing the next activity, also gives birth to a child that realizes there are some benefits to acting helpless.

The thought of being nagged to provide a "risk situation" for another, reminds me of an evening when the above concepts were being challenged at the home of a physician in Maine. I mentioned this story earlier in the text, and again because it illustrates human nature so accurately, therefore the following is offered in an abbreviated form, to illustrate the point.

Skeptical of the theory that "risk alone" stimulates the dormant sense of humor that lies within, the host was persistent that the "risk scenario" be provided for him, so that he might experience this "awakening." Reluctantly, I advised; "Go in and shave off your moustache." The dialogue that followed has left an indelible imprint.

"You mean to tell me, if I go in that bathroom and shave my moustache, it will enhance my sense of humor?" he questions with a broad grin.

"That's right."

"All I have to do, is get up, go in and shave these little black hairs off my face, and my sense of humor will begin to emerge?" he says with great zest.

"That's about the size of it." I offered.

"That's all I have to do, just shave?" He is now fully animated, with arms a flutter, offering gyrations, enthusiasm and possessing life with a spirit that few of us had ever witnessed before from him. All of this at the mere thought of shaving those little black hairs!

The room became fully spirited, as one physician offered another a suggestion as to what they might do in order to awaken this latent sense. Laughter, and back slapping were plentiful. If only there had been a camera available, those present, who would vaguely recall the experience in a few days, would have captured this moment of unguarded innocence.

If that physician were able to capture the essence of the moment, he would understand what his patients, and his peers yearn for when he walks into the examination or recovery room. The medical textbook would probably offer a paragraph of explanation under "bedside manner." We can't put our finger on it, but we know it when we see or experience it. It conveys an openness, and a receptiveness to others and their ideas.

What he had learned via textbook or practical experience, is that to be a physician, attorney, or dentist is serious business, and not to be approached too lightly. The public has expectations that must be met.

I can relate to my first appointment as a full-time faculty member, at Northern Michigan University. I went from full-time, practical, hands-on worker in the real world, to a member of a prestigious fraternity with a mystique that predates the hallowed ivy walls. What a responsibility I had.

I felt confident in my ability to teach, but I was concerned about the image I would portray to my students. I was relatively young for such an appointment, and unpublished, much to the dismay of my colleagues. However, a greater goal was to conquer the challenge of smoking prior to assuming my position on campus. After all, what sort of credibility would I have as a college instructor, if I didn't smoke a pipe? I did purchase the same, but never pursued it due to the embarrassment experienced when I apparently was indiscriminate in my choice of tobacco. Not cool.

This was a very meaningful experience, to capture and isolate the power and influence of society, my peers, and also the media. Trying to live up to the image of Peter O'toole, in "Goodbye Mr. Chips." Don't we all do that to a certain extent? The scary part is when we have completely sacrificed who we want to be, in order to be this person the world wants us to be. Frequently, we become so adept in our characterization, we no longer realize it's a facade. As a protective measure we fancy, this isn't who we really are, and we will drop the charade once our needs are met. Our resistance to dropping the facade intensifies because we are able to gain acceptance and "things" by effectively portraying someone we are not. Herein lies the enjoyment of associating with elderly people who have lived to expose the fraud that exists. Exposure to this truism is what made the movie "Cocoon", so enjoyable.

Reverting back to the meeting of physicians, did he shave the moustache? No. Did anyone think he would? No. Given a moment to regroup he was armed with all sorts of philosophical reasons why to do so would be inappropriate, and certainly not conclusive, in reference to my theory. It might also be added, that any suggestion of spontaneity, at the end of his discourse would certainly be of coincidence. He totally missed the point, but it wasn't lost on those who observed the exchange.

Even the existence of a moustache does not hold the status of independent thinking most of us would assume. "Middle America" did not support the presence of a moustache until 1972. In that year, an American hero appeared on the scene with a moustache. His prominence and status provided the permission, that allowed the rest of America to follow suit. Thank you, Olympian Mark Spitz.

His (the physician'), reluctance to shave was predictable, and symbolic. Symbolic in the sense that it represents our reluctance to change components or conditions affecting our lives, even if we are well aware it would be in our best interest to do so. Our moustaches stay, our hair styles stay, and our style of dress remain pretty much intact, and predictable. Our personalities are no exception, and will be addressed in a later chapter.

How often do we hear of marriages that end in divorce, and both parties admit it was dead fifteen years ago? People stay in jobs they hate until retirement! We continue to be bored with our existence and yet have not experimented with new associates, hobbies, or community groups. Frequently our willingness to experiment with new stimuli means switching to a different channel. And our willingness to do that, is influenced by the convenience of the remote. We become very predictable and stale.

With unlimited options, why return to the same location, year after year for vacation? Why do we take them within a two-day variance of last year's date? Why don't we read anything different, and subscribe to magazines that will broaden our perspective? Why do we sit in the same pew each week?

The reason is simple and sad. We may fail, therefore we don't. Rather than risk the failure we remain secure in what we know, good or bad. We prefer to whine, rather than will. The attempts we do make are frequently so grandiose, they are doomed for failure from the outset, and that also may be intentional. We may desire the comfort of saying how hard we tried in order to forgive our own continuance.

It's much easier to relate to the efforts to quit smoking, than to actually quit. Dieting continues to be an adaptation to the latest fad so that we may continue to be overweight, but comfortable in our explanations to prevent it. Individuals who are unhappy with their job, are extremely articulate in their discontent, but slow in their composition and distribution of their resume. Hard to explain in this day of word processing.

We are accountable to only one; ourself. And that accountability is usually not sufficient to motivate us to act. The weight of the socialization process is staggering, which is precisely why the risk taken must be in direct proportion to our willingness to accept defeat and continue. Even more importantly, in direct proportion to the certainty of our success. Don't underestimate how fragile we are. Studies indicate, two rejections will usually postpone continued attempts for a minimum of eighteen months, and most will not repeat the effort.

We become too cautious-and there is a need to restore some of the inner confidence that comes from taking risks. Examples of small risk are hazardous, given the wide range of individual response. Take a different route to work, park in a different location, eat lunch with someone new, talk openly with a stranger (two will benefit). The listing is endless, and the little risk should be encountered prior to the big ones. As indicated previously, who we are presently is a reflection of the choices that we have made given an uninterrupted sequence of events in our lives. Every situation holds the opportunity to take a risk. The most obvious risk, is whether to engage or not. For starters; those with a moustache, cut it. For those without, grow it. (This recommendation applies to both men and women).

SECTION 18

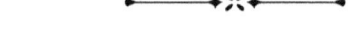

THE AFTERMATH

The Last Book … began with a proclamation that we had entered, and now exist within a perfect storm. This storm is not necessarily of our choosing, but we are a participant nevertheless. The purpose of this book was to identify the elements of the storm and then isolate the one trait, a sense of humor (openness, receptiveness to others, and their ideas), that is instrumental in aiding you in your passage through the storm; because there is a glimmer of a rainbow at the end.

The rainbow is the perfect metaphor to guide one through the storm. Just as it is sometimes difficult to see or identify precisely how or why you became the person you are, complete with very firm opinions and beliefs. So it is with the rainbow, an optical phenomenon caused by reflection. An electromagnetic spectrum of light that does not actually exist, but represents a sign of hope, the beauty after the storm. In current culture, the rainbow represents inclusivity and diversity, the antithesis of partisanship, a major component to the perfect storm in society,

Each of the different wave lengths within the spectrum of the rainbow are reflected at a different angle, analogous to the reality that each of us has different views and opinions based on our unique backgrounds, peer group and experiences. Given the unlimited variety and possibilities that exist contributing to the complexity of one's personal being, it is amazing that there is agreement or consensus about anything. Not to mention our willingness to force so many issues into an "either/or dynamic (partisan view).

In most instances, there are a variety of factors at play that contribute to a resolution of any situation under consideration. Just as the sun must be behind you and the clouds cleared away from the sun for the rainbow to appear. It is mind-boggling to suggest resolution lies within one of two options! And yet, this is how we, as a society, operate given our partisan orientation. Given our rainbow example, many would insist that it was necessary to have rain for a rainbow to exist. Science would tell us something else; rainbows may exist without rain and are referred to as a circumhorizontal arc's formed by ice crystals instead of rain.

It is this dichotomy of opinion, and insistence of being right, that creates so much frustration, anger and resentment among the populace. Instead of talking about rainbows I could have introduced the discussion relating to the appropriate response to Covid. No wait, I couldn't. This would immediately be the partisan divisor I wish to avoid.

I initially wanted to add a footnote to this discussion of the rainbow by adding a early reference to the rainbow from the Bible. (Please note: by mentioning that one reference point, I may have just crossed that imaginary line.) Whatever, we've come this far! In Genesis 9:13-15, God is speaking; "I set My rainbow in the cloud and it shall be a covenant between Me and the earth ... the waters shall never again become a flood to destroy all flesh."

The teaching moment is twofold: First, to point out at the subconscious level (partisan), how quickly some will discount what has been said, or will be said, as a result of the Christian reference. Secondly, to draw attention to the entire monologue of this section and demonstrate the need for one with a true sense of humor (nothing to do with jokes or comedy), demonstrating openness and a receptiveness to other's ideas is so instrumental to move the dialogue forward. In short, what is it worth to have one with this unique trait at the helm? Most would say priceless.

EPILOGUE

I entitled this book **The Last Book ...** because I believe if it truly isn't, it may be very close. I base this on a few conditions that didn't exist before. Or at least to the degree they do now. First, I believe book publishers will not be able to be profitable with the inevitably changing market that is transforming right before our eyes. This is a highly opinionated market that has very strong beliefs with little tolerance for dissenters. This lack of flexibility limits a significant portion of readers who were once tolerant or even curious about opposing opinions.

This sentiment reflects a variety of influences that are at play on potential readership. A major weight is the psychological need to belong to a supporting group. This need to belong has escalated recently, perhaps from the Covid experience requiring isolation, or perhaps from the technology that permits communication without talking or being physically present. We are seeking to belong to a group supporting the tenets of the group, as well as resisting those of the opposing view.

These opposing views are readily available. Time is of the essence, as it prompts one to choose a side and then invest in the defense of that side. This in turn narrows the scope of rationale and entrenches the isolation. The opportunity to just enjoy a good book is now provided by eBooks, or reduced to podcast summaries. In any event, none of the above reeks of good news for the publishing industry and we enter the realm of **The Last Book ...**

Because the technology transmitting text is forever present, it has an unintentional effect of making individuals always feel as if they are in demand to respond. Consequently, this pressure creates considerable anxiety. We attempt to compensate by responding with a menu of prepared options or emojis. The desired impact is lacking and the cycle repeats throughout the day and unfortunately, the night also.

At the risk of dating myself, I must admit these technical options were not available in my youth and I slept very soundly. I have lived a life that no man has a right to live and I wanted to document some of the influencer's that made that possible. Hopefully, I can gain the attention of my offspring briefly and reflect on these precious gems in order to make their short stay on this earth more pleasant and enjoyable. If some others benefit, all the better.

Due to my father's early influence, I have enjoyed leadership roles in sports, education and the corporate world. His influence was not only by example, he introduced me to Dale Carnegie and his work relating to effective communication, and the fundamental techniques in handling people. I felt like Indiana Jones as he gave me his dog-eared hard-back copy of *How to Win Friends and Influence People*. Margins on every page were flooded with insights and innuendoes that served as if they were clues on a treasure hunt. A table of contents that made me rush to deliver my morning papers so I could read chapters with titles like; "He Who Can Do This Has the Whole World with Him," "What Everybody Wants." And "Let the Other Peron Save Face."

I would ask my father, "Why doesn't everyone read this book?" He would just smile and explain how people are busy and have other priorities. Not a day passes when I don't witness nuggets of wisdom from that book. Yesterday no exception. I went to pay for a service that I inquired about a week earlier. This is a very modest business and setting and I had engaged with the salesperson for approximately an hour the previous week. Now ready to meet with her and sign a contract. She was occupied when I first entered so I waited for the opportunity to meet with her personally. I approached her desk and made a cordial greeting and she responded with, "And you are?" I immediately flashed back and recalled Carnegie's advice about how important a person's name is to them, and could attest to that first hand.

That brief experience yesterday with her not recalling my name is minor. It reminded me of how relevant some of these nuggets of advice from yesterday are. This is the motivation behind writing this book. It is the anticipation that the reader may glean a glimmer of insight as a result of my sharing some of the resources that I have been fortunate enough to encounter during my lifetime. I trust some reflections gathered over the years will benefit the reader.

The issue of engagement was upfront because in some respects it is the most challenged concept in the present work environment. An environment filled with self-interested, opinionated workers, threatened by advancing technologies and yet seeking an emotional commitment to the organization. Their dedication is limited if not recognized and rewarded with opportunities for growth. Any changes in policy without clear benefits for the employee is viewed as an attempt by management to gain some sort of an advantage.

Given the challenge of meeting the complex needs of the contemporary worker, the question then becomes what specific skills are necessary in order to meet and manage their demands? And just as important is what is the value to the organization for one who has those skills? Such people do exist and they come with a very high price tag. The benefits desired are realized. Within this personality makeup is a disposition that is very open and receptive to others and their ideas.

I flashback to teaching in the classroom in order to incorporate some of the dialog that reflects the concerns of the graduate student. They struggle to accurately define a true definition of humor and realize this sense if far more complex than comedy and jokes. Humor reflects a disposition and accompanying communication skills that are inherent in that disposition. Once the value of this trait is identified the benefits of maintaining it are discussed.

There is a search for the origin of this desirable trait. The secret sauce is found in one's self-esteem. The origin and the development, or in some cases the demise of self-esteem is revealed. Efforts pertaining to this development may be measured and evaluated on an hourly bases.

Recognizing that once the desired trait of a sense of humor, complete with the accompanying disposition is acquired, the challenge remains in communicating with diverse individuals. This is accomplished by initially matching emotional tones and moving forward to create a new reality. To exist and work in this state of harmony is to exist in the state of "FLOW" that can continue almost indefinitely.

This observation is challenged immediately reminding me of my question to my father, "Why isn't everyone reading this?" in reference to Carnegie's book. And the simple answer is, "For most people this would require change, and that is very difficult for most people." This desired change relates directly back to the hourly decisions referenced above. There is a certain irony with the introduction of contemporary technology as it relates to change. One would anticipate that technology would facilitate change. However, with that reality comes the opportunity that one may fail while attempting change and evidence of that failure lives on. Nothing worse than seeing the photos after regaining the weight loss.

The second half of the book is dedicated to reflecting on the research relating to isolating what traits or characteristics are unique to leaders that enables them to reduce conflict and move their organizations on to succeed. What is that skill worth to an organization?

The significance of a humorist disposition is provided by countless examples of primarily political figures and their ability to move their agenda forward utilizing this sixth sense. Given the importance of this trait considerable resources are dedicated to revealing where it comes from, what happens to it, and how may one regain it.

My journey of over twenty years has been a labor of love. It began decades before in early fireside chats with my father relating to persuasive communication. It benefitted me throughout my life as I employed many of the skills that would make my life more enjoyable and profitable.

I believe we are approaching more challenging times because the nature of our audience has changed. We advanced in our society because we were a compromising society. Today we are a partisan society, firm in our beliefs and our resistance. If we have to avoid, spin or lie in defense of our position; so be it. We have created a society that is artificial in our beliefs and our goals seeking immediate satisfaction. Our commitments are fragile and our attention spans are fleeting. We will weaponize our resources to achieve our ends at any cost.

Many would like to fold their tent and go home. Unfortunately, that's not an option. We must face the challenges put forth by society equipped with the resources needed to survive. It is the purpose of this book to provide a source of knowledge to make this possible. I wish you well.

PART IV

'ON MY WAY PROJECT'

ON MY WAY PROJECT

Given the current generation is having a great deal of difficulty stepping up to the plate and accepting any degree of responsibility for their behavior, I would like to look to the future, and focus on the youth of today.

Is there light at the end of the tunnel? Yes, there is and it is found in Section VII in the discussion involving self-esteem. Section VII outlines the development of self-esteem. We know that attitudes and behaviors are a reflection of one's self-esteem. We know self-esteem is a reflection of those critical choices or behaviors one makes along the way. It must ensue.

By way of review, life is a series or sequence of events and opportunities. These moments are continuous throughout a lifetime. These moments arise, and we make a choice, or choices, by combining the three behavioral options:

Maintain a Sharp Mental Focus or Drift;
Exercise Intellect or Emotions;
Utilize Your Own Judgement or The Judgement of Others.

For self-esteem to be enhanced one must choose the critical behaviors (CB's), that evolves from a sharp mental focus, is intelligent in its origin, and sponsored by the individual who will be affected.

Behaviors that result from mental drift are emotional in their makeup and are influenced by others and may be detrimental to the enhancement of self-esteem.

Obviously, there are numerous daily decisions that don't carry the weight of the world as a result of the action taken. Whether or not one eats a banana or an orange may not be impactful. However, a daily selection of a piece of fruit or a jelly-filled donut may have consequences over time. This is where the element of common sense plays a part. Unfortunately, that particular sense is not as common as one would hope.

Some people refer to these decisive moments as precipitating events, i.e. what happened or what thought process took place prior to your action? Note, the precipitating event may be positive or negative. Your reaction is what is critical. Successful people can list an entire sequence of events that were instrumental in their success and they write about that in their autobiographies. Self-esteem is acquired due to action and behaviors, not bestowed or given by someone else. Follow behaviors, they become the blueprints for self-esteem.

As previously suggested, unsuccessful people will also provide an ample list. This will be a listing of victimizing people and statements that are responsible for their failures. And they may be very articulate in stating them. They have rehearsed these explanations for years. In some respects, this represents the state of drift mentioned previously. 'Drifting' is a negative state of mind conspicuous by its emptiness of purpose.

The **'ON MY WAY' project'** will address the development and enhancement of high or positive self-esteem directly. It is my intention to have the youth of today fully realize they are the architects of their own destiny. This destiny is built on the decisions and behaviors they manifest on a daily. These decisions become the building blocks of positive self-esteem. Self-esteem is an individual's subjective evaluation of their own worth. If and to the extent that one lacks self-esteem, they feel driven to fake it, commonly referred to as pseudo selfesteem. The reality is, control your own destiny or someone else will.

ENGAGEMENT...for an eight-year-old would begin with a thorough explanation of terms and definitions relating to self-esteem and the role it plays in development and achievement of goals in life.

This will be facilitated by flash cards and class discussion. A mini-journal to record self-esteem efforts will be distributed and a board game that demonstrates progress will be introduced. The teacher maintains custodial privilege over all efforts. Periodically, the child will transfer the journal listings and board-game progress to an autobiographical, hard covered book entitled, "On My Way." This book is also available on disk and is a keepsake, complete with pictures if desired, and the sole property of the student.

The hard copy may be printed at the suggested conclusion date (twelve-years of age), or any time during the self-esteem exercise. The entire project continues as the student matriculates to the next grade level. The concepts underlying positive self-esteem will be well established at this time. It is anticipated that many students will continue with journal and/or disk entries for years to come.

Learning Styles…are primarily visual, auditory and kinesthetic. The 'On My Way 'project incorporates all three learning styles therefore catering to the desired learning style of the individual.

ASSESSMENT

WHAT IF…the concept of self-esteem is introduced at a very early age? Perhaps the age of eight years. This suggested age would allow a certain degree of common sense and judgement to be present, as well as verbal skills, and hopefully, prior to a variety of negative influences. For those skeptics who insist it is already too late, I would suggest an ambitious plan of corrective action utilizing the formula above. These turn-around efforts can be very rewarding to the parties involved. Most significantly, youth have not refined their level of justification, denial or rebuttal that the parents have.

IMAGINE IF YOU WILL…an entire family that engaged periodically in this review of selected behaviors. Now I don't live in a cloud I realize that train of intact families has left the station. It is nice to dream. This is why I feel this effort must be handled within the school system, preferably at the third-grade level.

CONCEIVE OF A SCHOOL SYSTEM…comprised of a student body that is well versed in discussions relating to incidents that required a sharp mental focus, intellect or personal judgement.

CONSIDER…an entire school system and community that is well versed in the efforts necessary to achieve positive self-esteem and achieve personal and professional goals.

WHO BENEFITS…in addition to the individual? Each family member related and associated with an individual with high self-esteem benefits from their example. Every mental health agency in the community that deals with anxiety, depression, suicide, alcohol and drug abuse, and domestic abuse benefits from a population of high self-esteem individuals. Every agency affiliated with the criminal justice system benefits from a population of high self-esteemed individuals due to a decrease in populations representing probationers, paroles, and incarcerated individuals. Health providers are free to focus on individuals with serious health problems opposed to patients experiencing health problems that are self-imposed by definition. School administrators and counselors are free to focus on educational needs.

APPENDIX A

'ON MY WAY'

The 'On My Way' project is a companion to the *book; Bridging the Communication Gap* by author James Haviland. The intent of the project is to present the materials in Sections VI and VII in the book in a manner catering to a more youthful audience. Both sections deal with the origins and maintenance of self-esteem. This project will require a more interactive engagement than that of the adult reader. The focus is for an audience of eight to twelveyears, or third to sixth grade.

The major premise of the project is to enhance and create an awareness of one's 'self-esteem' by recognizing their role in elevating the same. Self-esteem is a subjective evaluation or opinion of ones' own worth. Self-esteem is the opinion one has of oneself. There is no value-judgement more important to an individual than the estimate they pass on themselves. This determination is made by the individual and subsequently influences their behavior. The purpose of this project is for an individual to record specific behaviors enacted that will enhance their own self-esteem and encourage them 'On Their Way' to becoming the successful person they desire to be.

The project requires a notebook for journal entries, a Building Bridges Board (3B) with stickers, and eventually an avenue to publish the beginning chapters of an autobiography. The autobiography will be a hardbound book reflecting life experiences to accompany the early critical behaviors that contribute to a positive self-esteem. This book may be published at the end of the third grade of school or postponed until the completion of a school project that will continue through sixth grade.

The project board has a unisex silhouette in the middle with the caption 'On My Way'. Radiating out from the silhouette are eight avenues of exit, each having a cobble stone bridge midway. The bridge provides an opportunity to lay thirty to fifty paving stones. The eight exits are located on the four corners of the board and midway on each side. The exits are labeled; Friendships, Hobbies, Acts of Kindness, *Occupation, Volunteer Work, Savings, Fitness & Health and Education.

*Occupation may refer to current efforts reflected by allowance, paper routes etc. It may also reflect time invested in researching possible careers that are of interest. This may be an expressed interest in becoming a professional athlete, airline pilot, attorney etc. or interviewing the same to gain insight to the profession.

The journals are identified by the 'On My Way' silhouette sticker provided and self-applied. The journal is also divided by the student into eight sections corresponding with the eight exits on the Building Bridges Board. Stickers identifying the eight exits are also provided. Each entry in the section shall begin with the date and a listing of the self-esteem activity that took place. The student then transfers one cobble stone sticker to the bridge that corresponds with the appropriate exit. This represents visual confirmation of their efforts to become the person they want to be.

Once this has been completed a check mark is placed next to the journal entry to indicate the cobble stone has been placed on the board. At the end of the school year or periodically during the school year, the student records the efforts they have put forth to reach their individual goals by making a computer entry to their autobiography. This entry is produced in hardback copy at the time of their choosing. Ideally this will be at the end of the fouryear project. This visual documentation instills in them personal pride, elevates self-esteem and provides concrete evidence to them that they are 'On Their Way' to becoming the person they want to be. Realizing you are the architect of your own destiny, what a precious keepsake.

> *"Life isn't about finding yourself. Life is about creating yourself."*
> *-George Bernard Shaw*

APPENDIX B

'ON MY WAY TUTORIAL'

*This entire session between the tutor (T) and the student (S) may be taped for prosperity. Director (D).

T: Do you know what self-esteem is?
S: No.
T: Do you know what an opinion is?
S: The way you think? D: Coach them to accepting this definition via numerous examples. T: Let's do some examples. What is your favorite sports team, television program, subject, color etc.
T: Why do you like that particular one? S: Explains.
T: Is that every ones' favorite? S: No.
T: What you have said about your favorite may or may not be true, but it is what you believe to be true? S: Yes. T: This is what an opinion is. Your best guess as to what is true.
T: Let's go back to the word esteem. Esteem simply means highly or favorable opinion. So, what would the word self-esteem mean?
S: It would be my opinion of myself. T: BINGO!
T: So, let me ask? What is your self-esteem, or opinion of yourself and why? D: In the event the responses start to be negative, redirect

them to the fact 'esteem' is favorable. D: You may wish to write their responses down briefly.
T: If you wanted to raise your self-esteem or your opinion of yourself what would you have to do?
S: I would have to do good or positive things.
T: Could you give me some examples of what you might do? D: Let them go and try to remember those that directly relate to the Building Bridges Board; Friendships, Hobbies, Acts of Kindness, Occupation*, Volunteer Work, Savings, Fitness & Health, and Education. D: See prompt questions APPENDIX C.

*Occupation may relate to current responsibilities like paper routes, raking leaves or chores granting allowance. It may also reflect time spent researching occupations to which they have expressed an interest. Interviews of individuals currently or previously employed in that occupation may also be considered.

'ON MY WAY PROJECT'

STAGE TWO

Once the student is clear regarding the definition and how one raises self-esteem (positive behaviors that enhance one's opinion of self), introduce the option of recording by date, the actual behavior that takes place. This will require a journal that has been divided into the eight categories represented on the Building Bridges Board.

At the appropriate time, the journal entry will be transferred (via sticker or coloring) to the Building Bridges Board for a visual representation of progress. At this step in the process, it may serve as a time to share experiences that have taken place within the desired areas of development.

Midway or at the conclusion of the school year the students will reflect on their progress that has occurred and blend these positive results with other events that have taken place like a summer family trip etc. These biographical events will be published in a computerized hard cover book entitled 'On My Way'. Each student will have their own hard-covered book, and if desired by the student the publishing may be postponed until the same process is repeated the following year(s). The end result will be a critical awareness on the part of the child during their formative years of the role they play in developing their self-esteem and becoming the type of person they desire to be.

"Life isn't about finding yourself. Life is about creating yourself."
-George Bernard Shaw

APPENDIX C

PROMPTS FOR BUILDING BRIDGES BOARD CATEGORIES

Friendships
    New Students
    Neighbors
    Correspondence

Hobbies
    Pets
    Activities
    Lessons

Acts of Kindness
    Helping Others
    Visiting Seniors
    Animal Support

Occupation
    Current Responsibilities (allowance related)
    Researching Future Opportunities
    Interviewing Previously Employed

Volunteer Work
    With Elderly
    Outside of Home
    With Families in Need

Savings
    From Current Allowance
    Gifts Received
    Bank Savings Account

Fitness & Health
    Current Exercise Program
    Eating Habits
    Organized Activity

Education
    Attendance
    Outside of School Educational Programs
    Lessons of Instruction/Information

PART V

RESOURCES

RESOURCES

Ailes, Roger, with Jon Kraushar. *You Are The Message: Secrets of the Master Communicators.* Homewood, Illinois: Dow Jones-Irwin, 1988.

Arluke, A. and Levin, J. Gossip: The Inside Scoop.

Barreca, Regina. *They Used to Call Me Snow White...but I Drifted.* New York: Penguin Books, 1991.

Bauby, Jean-Dominique. *The Diving Bell and the Butterfly: A Memoir of Life Death.* New York: Vintage Press, 1997.

Bellah, Robert. *Habits of the Heart.* Berkeley: University of California Press, 1985.

Bennett, William J. *The Book of Virtues.* New York: Simon and Schuster, 1993.

Bennis, Warren. *Why Leaders Can't Lead.* San Francisco: Jossey-Bass, 1990.

Bloom, Allan. *The Closing of the American Mind.* New York: Simon and Schuster, 1987.

Branden, Nathaniel. *The Psychology of Self-Esteem: 1969, Breaking Free:1970. The Disowned Self:1972,* Los Angeles: Nash Publishing Corporation. *The Power of Self-Esteem.* New York: Barnes & Noble, 2001.

Buscaglia, Leo. *Living, Loving & Learning.* New York: Holt, Rinehart and Winston, 1982.

Canfield, Jack. *The Success Principles.* New York: Harper Collins Publishers, 2005.

Carnegie, Dale. *How to Win Friends and Influence People.* Dale Carnegie and Associates Inc. Hauppauge, NY. 1936.

Clark, Karen Kaiser. Life Is Change *Growth Is Optional.* St. Paul Minnesota:

Csikszentmihalyi, Mihaly. *Good Business.* New York: Penguin Group, 2003.

Csikszentmihalyi, Mihaly. *FLOW: The Psychology of Optimal Experience.* New York: Harper & Row, Publishers, 1990.

DePree, Max. *Leadership Is An Art.* New York: Doubleday, 1989

Dyer, Wayne. *Your Erroneous Zones.* New York: Avon Books, 1976.

Eadie, Betty. *Embraced By The Light.* Onjinjinkta Distribution, 1992. Redfield, James. *The Celestine Prophecy.* New York: Warner Books, 1993. Bellah, Robert. *Habits of the Heart. Berkeley:* University of California Press, 1985.

Freud, Sigmund. *Jokes and Their Relations to the Unconscious.* New York: Norton, 1960.

Funk, Wilfred. *Word Origins and Their Romantic Stories.*

Gardner, Gerald. *All The Presidents' Wits: The Power of Presidential Hum. 1986.*

Gerzon, Mark. *Choice of Heroes*: *The Changing Face of American Manhood.* Houghton Mifflin Company, 1992.

Goleman, Daniel. *Working with Emotional Intelligence.* New York: Bantam Books, 1998.

Hill, Napoleon. *Law of Success.* Chicago: Success Unlimited, Inc., MCMLXXIX.

Hill, Napoleon. *Outwitting the Devil: The Secret to Freedom and Success.* New York: Sterling Publishing Co., Inc. 2011.

Himmelfarb, Gertrude. *On Looking Into the Abyss:Untimely Thoughts on Culture and Society.*

Hunter, James C., *The Servant:A Simple Story About the True Essence of Leadershp.* Roseville, CA: Prima Publishing, 1998.

Iacocca, L. *and* Novak, W., *Iacocca: An Autobiography.* New York: Bantam Books, 1984.

Jaworski, Joseph. *Synchronicity*. Berrett-Koehler Publishers. San Francisco. *1996*.

Karsan, Rudy and Kruse, Kevin. **WE**: *How To Increase Performance and Profits Through Full Engagement*. Hoboken, New Jersey, John Wiley & Sons Inc, 2011.

Kaufman, Scott B. "The Peacock Paradox," *Psychology Today*," August 2011, 56.

Klein, Allen. *The Healing Power of Humor*. New York: G.P. Putnam's Sons, 1989.

Kotter, John P. *The Heart of Change*. Harvard Business School Press. Boston, MA. 2002.

Kruse, Kevin. *Employee Engagement 2.0*. Richboro, PA: The Kruse Group, 2012.

Langelett, George, *How Do I Keep My Employees Motivated? The Practice of Empathy-Based Management*. Austin, TX: River Grove Books, 2014.

Leider, Richard. and Shapiro, David. *Repacking Your Bags: Lighten Your Load for the Rest of Your Life*. Berrett-Koehler Publishers, Incorporated, 1995.

Lencioni, Patrick. *The Five Dysfunctions of a Team*. Jossey-Bass, San Francisco, CA. 2002.

Lester, Julius. "Whatever Happened to the Civil Rights Movement?" as cited in Sykes, Charles A. *A Nation of Victims: The Decay of the American Character*. New York: St. Martin's Press, 1992.

Maltz, Maxwell. *Psycho-Cybernetics (updated Edition)*. Fine Communications, 2002.

Marsh, Abigail. *The Fear Factor: How One Emotion Connects Altruists, Psychopaths, & Everyone In-Between*. New York: Hachette Book Group, 2017.

Maslow, Abraham H. "The Jonah Complex", as cited in *Interpersonal Dynamics*. Homewood, Illinois: The Dorsey Press, 1968.

Maslow, Abraham H., *Motivation and Personality*, Harper & Row, New York, 1954

McGhee, Paul. *Humor:Its Origin and Development*. San Francisco: W.H. Freeman and Company, 1979.

Milea, Jinx. *Why Jenny Can't Lead*.

Mindess, Harvey. *Laughter and Liberation.* Los Angeles, California: Nash Publishing, 1971.
Minshull, Ruth. *How To Choose Your People.* Scientology. Ann Arbor, MI 1972.
Naisbitt, John. *Megatrends.* New York: Warner Books, 1982.
Olson, Rick J. and Strand, Robert. *Unleash Your Greatness: Become a Person of Impact.* Richmond, Virginia, 2002.
Peele, Stanton. *The Diseasing of America.* San Francisco: Lexington Books, 1995.
Putnam, Robert. *Bowling Alone.* New York: Simon and Schuster, 2000. Himmelfarb, Gertrude. *On Looking Into the Abyss: Untimely Thoughts on Culture and Society.*
Redfield, James. *The Celestine Prophecy.* New York: Warner Books, 1993.
Ringer, Robert A. *Restoring the American Dream.* QED Publishing. New York, NY. 1979.
Schieffer, B. and Gates, G.P. *The Acting President: Ronald Reagan & the Supporting Players Who Helped Him Create the Illusion That Held America Spellbound.* 1990.
Smiles, Samuel. *SELF-HELP.* London: John Murray, 1859.
Storr, Will. *Selfie: How we Became So Self-Obsessed and What It's Doing to Us.* New York: The Overlook Press, Peter Mayer Publishers, Inc. 2018.
Sykes, Charles J. *A Nation of Victims.* New York: St. Martin's Press, 1992.
Tannen, Deborah. *You Just Don't Understand.* New York: Ballentine Books, 1990.
Tenge, Jean M. and Campbell, W. Keith. *The Narcissism Epidemic.* New York: Simon & Schuster, 2009.
Trueblood, Eldon. *The Humor of Christ. 1975.*
Twenge, Jean. and Campbell, Keith. *The Narcissism Epidemic.* Atria, Simon & Schuster. New York, NY. 2009.
Ventura, Jesse. *I Ain't Got Time to Bleed: Reworking the Body Politic from the Bottom Up.*
Webber, Rebecca. "The Real Narcissists," *Psychology Today,*" October 2016, 51.

Wyden, Peter. *The Unknown Iacocca. 1987.*
Zunin, Natalie. *Contact:The First Four Minutes.* New York: Ballantine Books, 1972.
Zweig, David. *Invisibles; The Power of Anonymous Work in an age of Relentless Self-Promotion.* Penguin Group (USA) LLC. New York. 2014